THE MEANING OF
THE MARK

By the Same Author:

IT WORKS!

*The famous little red book containing
a workable plan that enables you
to realize your heart's desire.*

THE MEANING OF THE MARK

The Miracle Mark of Omar

Adopted as his Guide to Health, Wealth and Happiness

In Three Versions

BY

R. H. J.

Author of "It Works"

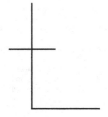

JEREMY P. TARCHER/PENGUIN
a member of Penguin Group (USA)
New York

JEREMY P. TARCHER/PENGUIN
Published by the Penguin Group
Penguin Group (USA), 375 Hudson Street,
New York, New York 10014, USA

USA · Canada · UK · Ireland · Australia
New Zealand · India · South Africa · China

Penguin Books Ltd, Registered Offices: 80 Strand, London WC2R 0RL, England
For more information about the Penguin Group visit penguin.com

The Meaning of the Mark was originally published in 1931 by the Larger Life Library.
First Tarcher/Penguin edition published 2013.

Library of Congress Cataloging-in-Publication Data

Jarrett, R. H. (Roy Herbert), date.
The meaning of the mark : the miracle mark of Omar, adopted as his
guide to health, wealth and happiness : in three versions / by R. H. J.,
author of "It works". — First Tarcher/Penguin edition.
p.   cm.
"The Meaning of the Mark was originally published in 1931 by the
Larger Life Library."
ISBN 978-0-399-16446-0
1. New Thought. I. Title.
BF639.J43   2013   2013015302
131—dc23

Book design by Meighan Cavanaugh

CONTENTS

VERSION III.

INTRODUCTION

This book is the record of an experiment in larger life. The elements of the experiment were blood and tears, bone and muscle and other significant factors such as heartaches, aspirations, weariness, dumb fear, blind hope and soaring joyousness. These common elements of human nature compounded through a period of many years produced a man—a man with a philosophy, a purpose and a message.

His message found expression in the form of a modest but vital book entitled "It Works!" This was his first book; he made no claim to authorship but he could not refrain from telling others of the plan that had given him health, wealth, happiness and more perfect self-expression.

On the front cover appeared a mark, simple in design

but profound in meaning. It was the mark of the cross and square which, although not mentioned or explained in the text, nevertheless attracted attention and was really the undisclosed reason for the book. This mark was the focus of the author's thought, and summed up the central idea of his extraordinary book.

"It Works!" became the guide and handbook of a multitude of earnest men and women seeking more abundant life. It spurred them on to a venture of faith, supplied them with a concise plan for eliminating wrong ideas and establishing right ones. In the lives of thousands it demonstrated the transforming power of divine energy.

To these people the mark provided a convenient reminder of their new vision. Some adopted it as a personal symbol. Copies of "It Works!" by the hundreds were bought and given away as a practical means of sharing with friends the blessings and benefits derived. Wherever the book went the mark of the cross and square was seen on the cover and its meaning if not understood, was at least surmised by many.

Great numbers wrote the author in gratitude and enthusiasm for the change that was wrought in their lives. It was the conviction of those who were privileged to read these letters that there was need for another book of wider scope developing and emphasizing the spiritual implications as well as the practical aspects of this philosophy of soul power and material prosperity. Such a course would scatter the good news inherent in the mark to a much wider audience and remove all chance of anyone missing its full message.

The simple mark of the cross and square seemed much too big to risk leaving it on the cover of a book without comment. It clamored to be put inside a book of its own, to be written out, explained, indeed proclaimed as the theme and consummation of a resounding credo.

Consequently it was urged upon the author as an opportunity and an obligation that he undertake the larger venture of this present volume to fully explain the meaning of this mystic mark which has such far-flung power to make over lives when its significance was comprehended and applied.

As you read these pages you will see how ably this task

has been done. Here in three versions or interpretations is given a vivid and fascinating exposition of the meaning of this mysterious, potent mark. The fullness of its meaning spans the spread from humble earth to highest heaven, ties the finite to the infinite and lifts the remotest reach of human life to the throne of God.

December 1st, 1930
Jewell F. Stevens

AUTHOR'S FOREWORD

It is my prayer and confident hope that the reading of this book may impart new power and greater prosperity, and that Paul Omar's price mark of success may become the life mark of many people.

The popular tendency will doubtless be to accept this mark and employ its influence for the sake of temporal benefit. Such a course is quite proper but there is much more than this to the mark.

It is the embodiment of an eternal truth. It proclaims the true relationship between God and man. Jesus summed up the Law in terms of its meaning—honor God and serve man. The angels of the plains of Bethlehem chorused its supreme significance in the song that the ages will always echo, "Glory to God in the highest, and on earth peace, good will toward men." It is this higher ideal that is of vital importance.

Because of the age-long truth embodied in the meaning of this mark I take no personal credit for this book except for the opportunity of writing it down and even this would have been most arduous if not impossible without the kind help of many friends and the advantage of wide contacts that have provided me so generously with material, incidents and examples.

Especially I appreciate the unflagging interest and helpfulness which the publishers have shown in suggesting editorial revisions that have clarified the text. Also am I grateful to Theresa Gustafson for the typing of the manuscript and to Angela M. Crawley for the reading of the proofs.

As in the case of my former book, It Works, I prefer to be known only by my initials.

November 15th, 1930
R. H. J.

THE TIN GEE GEE

In a Toy Shop

Then the little tin soldier he sobbed and he sighed,
So I patted his little tin head.
"What vexes your little tin soul?" said I,
And this is what he said:
"I've been on this stall a very long time,
And I'm marked twenty-nine, as you see;
Whilst just on the shelf above my head,
There's a fellow marked sixty-three."

"Now he hasn't got a sword and he hasn't got a horse,
And I'm quite as good as he.
So why mark me at twenty-nine,
And him at sixty-three?
There's a pretty little dolly girl over there,

And I'm madly in love with she.
But now that I'm only marked twenty-nine,
She turns up her nose at me.
She turns up her little wax nose at me,
And carries on with sixty-three."
"Cheer up, my little tin man," said I,
"I'll see what I can do.
You're a fine little fellow, and it's a shame
That she should so treat you."
So I took down the label from the shelf above,
And I labeled him "Sixty-three,"
And I marked the other one "twenty-nine,"
Which was very, very wrong of me,
But I felt so sorry for that little tin soul,
As he rode on his tin Gee Gee.

Now that little tin soldier he puffed with pride,
At being marked sixty-three.
And that saucy little dolly girl smiled once more,
For he'd risen in life, you see.

—Fred Cape

VERSION

I

I

A MYSTERIOUS IMPULSE

Y ou may put down three million dollars as Mr. Omar's contribution to this endeavor," quietly remarked the young secretary to the group of business men seated around the table in a private dining room at the Union League Club.

THREE MILLION DOLLARS was said as easily as most men would say "thirty cents" and was, indeed, a small sum of money when compared with previous contributions of many millions which Paul Omar had made to various worthy projects for the betterment of mankind.

Bewilderment and surprise flashed over the faces of those sincere men. They were temporarily stunned. A terrific noiseless explosion would have caused the same effect. Three million dollars! True, they were all fairly-well-to-do, prosperous men. On an average, their incomes were about thirty thousand a year. One hundred thousand dollars would have been a magnificent start on the Five-Million-Housing-Plan Fund; but THREE MILLION!—three-fifths of all they needed—coming from ONE MAN! The very thought of it was almost inconceivable, especially to Frank Barnard, the youngest and one of the most active of the group.

"Where and how did Paul Omar get all those millions? How did it feel to *give away* such an enormous sum? Would he tell me the secret?" These were the selfish thoughts which flashed through Barnard's mind as he looked at that unassuming man sitting there next to his secretary. Barnard watched Paul Omar closely. He sensed an unusualness about the man—some quality entirely different from anyone he had ever met. The questions about his money were forgotten in the overwhelming desire to know what made Paul Omar so different from other men. What was the mysterious power he had which the others did not have or were not able to harness? What was "that something" that made this man an outstanding personality? Barnard yearned to know and possess it for himself. It was something far greater than the knowledge of material values. It seemed a "sureness" as to the purpose of life. "Absence of fear" would not define it, as fear, apparently, had never existed for him.

Paul Omar was *sure*—that was his chief characteristic. His actions and his conversation indicated his sureness. For example, Barnard remembered his remark about Lindbergh, "THE SUCCESS OF LINDBERGH WAS DUE TO THE SOUL DESIRE OF A MAJORITY."

Barnard had not the least idea what he meant but he did know this remarkable man was sure of what he said.

During this trend of thought, Barnard caught the kindly, loving look of Paul Omar turned on him and it seemed to say, "Come to me. I'll gladly tell you what I meant and many other things that are now troubling you. Come and learn my secret and you, too, may become an outstanding personality—a power among your associates."

That persistent, mysterious impulse possessed Barnard for the remainder of the day. It seemed to whisper, "Go and see Omar. Your opportunity is at hand." Then common sense would war with intuition and suggest the absurdity of such a visit.

Several times in the night he awakened with the feeling that Paul Omar was present in his room. Through sleep-drugged senses he could hear Omar talking—explaining his secret.

About eleven o'clock the next morning, finding it impossible to disregard this ever-conscious urge, Barnard left his office and took a taxi to Omar's office, with the intention of making an appointment for a future interview. He presented his card and was greatly astounded when the clerk returned and said, "Mr. Omar was expecting you. Step right in."

When the door closed and he was alone with the man who intrigued his imagination and interest by giving away three million dollars on the previous day, Barnard was plainly embarrassed.

Mr. Omar's kindly greeting and his cordial urge to take the comfortable chair beside the desk, helped little to abate the embarrassment. He was here—in Omar's office—but why?

Paul Omar waited and finally said, "Well?"

That "Well" brought Barnard to the realization that he must speak. Haltingly he began, "Mr. Omar, some unknown force has compelled me to visit you. Your personality—your manner—you are a remarkable man. I want to be like you—what is it that makes you so different—so outstanding—such a power—so remarkable?"—here his voice failed him and he could say no more.

Omar did not answer him immediately but just smiled that kindly, powerful smile. "I knew you would come to me. I'm glad you did." Then abruptly he asked, "By the way, have you ever read 'The Tin Gee Gee'?"

Upon receiving a negative reply, Omar recited the entire poem with the smile of retrospection lingering on his face. "The beginning of what you want to know happened many years ago—when I was re-marked from twenty-nine cents to sixty-three. It happened almost as quickly as did the re-marking of the little tin soldier in the toy shop."

All embarrassment was gone. This man who could give away millions was extremely human. He could talk about changing the price on a toy soldier and had said that he himself once had been marked as low as "twenty-nine cents."

"What a change since then," laughed Barnard. "You need no price mark *now*—everybody *knows* it."

Omar's face became grave, "I wish they did," he said, musingly. Looking at Barnard intently and with a slight hesitancy of speech, he continued, "Yes, there is still a price mark. It is in code—few understand it. You cannot decipher it now. But as I know your desire and the purpose of your visit to be sincere, and because I understand the mysterious power which sent you here, communicating to me your intentions, I will gladly give you the price mark placed on TRUE HAPPINESS AND WORLDLY WEALTH."

Taking a pencil in his hand he made this mark:

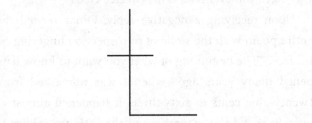

Out of this visit grew many interesting, enjoyable and profitable evenings, some sessions lasting until the small hours of the morning. These evenings with Paul Omar gave Frank Barnard:

A new conception of God's Law of Possession,

A definite reason and purpose for his life on this earth,

A positive assurance of life hereafter, and a symbol—sign—or mark, to guide and strengthen him: the mysterious price mark.

To decipher this mark and cherish it in your heart, you, like Barnard, must gather and kindle the thought fagots scattered through this volume.

> *"What is all knowledge but recorded experience, and a product of history; of which therefore, reasoning and belief, no less than action and passion, are essential materials?"*
>
> —CARLYLE

II

A TERSE ROMANCE OF ACTION AND PASSION

> *"Romances, in general, are calculated rather to fire the imagination than to inform the judgment."*
>
> —RICHARDSON

Years before, Paul Omar, an orphan, known as "Ivan Levine," was an apprentice in the shipyards at Seattle. His associates were Anarchists or Reds, leagued together against Capital—as they termed it—"Capital" meaning any one who hired and paid Labor. In frenzy and with much gesticulation, they talked of the unfairness in the distribution of Money and Power, predicting a time when Labor would become strong enough to rise up and control Capital. They gloated over the thought of how wonderful it would be when the tables were turned—when Labor could loaf and Capital—meaning moneyed men—would sweat as did Labor now.

Ivan, being just a boy, wanted money and power, too. His constant passion was to get ahead; but the childhood lessons of Father Abraham and Moses were an integral part of his life and seemed out of harmony with the proposed method to getting rich by revolution. His common sense questioned this proposed method.

Then came that great day when Capital, from the East, came to Seattle in a private car to meet and talk with Labor. Great was the excitement in the Red ranks. Here, at last, was their chance to take a rap at Capital. They were not strong enough for violence but they could show their contempt. This they would do; and their plan was to break up the evening meeting by continuous and uncalled-for applause. No one could tell who started it; they would be safe from blame; and what a huge joke it would be! Ivan fell in with the plan. Everybody seemed to be for it, but when the time came, a miracle happened. The big guy called Charlie, representing Capital, stood up, smiled, and said, "Howdy, Fellows!" Instantly, every man was with him and *for* him. The speech and the smile continued, broken only by sincere and unusually short applause. Ivan did not understand what he said but he felt that he had found a friend. A passion to be like this man with the wonderful smile, to live as he lived, to have what he had, including the private car, took possession of Ivan's heart.

Then another miracle happened. The *price tag* on Ivan Levine was changed. He was on the private car, speeding back to Pittsburgh with his new friend, who had promised to give him an education.

At Yale, because of his love for astronomy, he was dubbed "Omar" by many of his student friends; while others, in a vein of humor, generated by his appearance and demeanor, nicknamed him "Saint Paul."

Four years later, following his application and prayer to the Circuit Court, Judge Graham signed the petition giving him the name of Paul Omar, now known throughout the country.

Like Saul of Tarsus and Omar Khayyam, those tent makers of old, builders of homes which gave comfort to humanity, Paul Omar in this Twentieth century has fashioned a tent of curious design, housing and comforting thousands of human souls.

Like Khayyam, he sought for truth and, later, like Saint Paul, he found it to such a degree that he could say with all the assurance of understanding, "This is my way—the way."

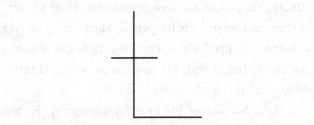

This mysterious symbol is the price mark of knowledge, wealth, happiness and truth.

III

REASONING AND BELIEF

"A hair perhaps divides the False and True;
Yes, and a single Alif were the clue—
Could you but find it—to the Treasure-house,
And peradventure to the Master, too;

"I sent my Soul through the Invisible,
Some letter of that After-life to spell;
And by and by my Soul return'd to me,
And answer'd, "I Myself am Heav'n and Hell."

Poor old learned Omar Khayyam! How close he came to the truth—within a hair's thickness—but failed to reason it out. His Soul whispered unto him, "I am Heaven and Hell"; but he could not grasp the idea that his Soul *might be* THE GOD-GIVEN, INDEPENDENT, EARTHLY POWER, often called the "subconscious mind," which guides our destiny and makes us what we are; that expression of the law of God which gives to man his true desire—the things he thinks of, longs for, expects or dreads the most; that power which shows you the way, brings to pass and MAKES A REALITY of your dominant thought.

Paul Omar smiled at the expression on Barnard's face. "Do not be so serious, my dear friend," he said. "You cannot force your reason to accept these facts which I have proved to myself for so many years. The acceptance will, I hope, eventually come to you; but for the present, simply endeavor to understand what I say. Get the fundamentals. Never mind about the truth of the statements. Joubert wrote something like this: 'There is a malignant reason which delights in the errors it succeeds in discovering; that unfeeling and scornful reason which insults credulity.'

"Most of us have an abundance of this sort of reasoning. In fact, we try to *compel* reason—something which cannot be done. I do not expect you at once to believe what I am telling you but will be satisfied if you can comprehend my belief. Later on, you may choose *what* to believe.

"God Himself elects to be served by choice—not by

compulsion. His law compels man to work out his own destiny and nothing can change this law. Faith and doubt are voluntary acts. Freewill is one of the conditions attached to human life. You must choose by thought, word and deed, and what you elect to do God will not prevent. The choice is yours. What greater gift could you ask? God is good; and by this very law man may rise to the greatest heights or sink to the lowest depths.

"The dominating thought of man's objective mind (the mind you use every day) is transferred to man's Soulpower, which infallibly acts as directed. *This moment* your life is exactly what You have made it and tomorrow will be what you *make* it. Your present material worth is as you planned and your happiness or sorrow as you made it—by choice. 'But,' one might say, 'it was not my choice. I wanted this or that and did not get it.' The answer is, he got exactly what he expected. Another might say, 'If all this is true, I may obtain anything I want very easily just by thinking about it.' The answer to this is—not easily, but *surely*.

"Merely saying something is by no means thinking it. So often you say one thing and think the opposite or, like the eight-year-old boy betting a million dollars, you do not think at all.

"A man who verbally swears may not be taking God's

name in vain any more than the man saying the Lord's Prayer may be praying. Thinking is far more than making a noise. In fact, noises of all kinds, including loud talking, greatly interfere with thinking. Reading is an aid to thought but writing your thoughts is of immeasurable benefit to well-founded, organized and definite reasoning.

"'I could be arrested for what I am thinking,' is jokingly said by people who do not know the potent power of thought and think only what they *do* is of importance; but every man's actions and deeds are the DIRECT RESULT OF THE WAY HE THINKS.

"'As a man thinketh, so is he.'

"As the soul directs, desires become realities and no morals or codes of any people are incorporated in this basic law. This is God's law, not man's law.

"The Old Testament is full of proof that at the fall of man, his power of achievement was not taken from him. God seemed to have said, 'You would not be governed by My judgment when all was well with you; now use your own and see what happens. Learn by experience that the false and corrupt will be swept away. Discover, if you will, what truth is, for truth alone shall last forever. Seek and ye shall find, even unto My judgment and help, if that be your true desire; but I will not compel it. You must do so of your own will. Yours is the choice.'"

What a privilege it was to listen to this man so firmly grounded, who stated his opinions so simply, so calmly, so frankly; who made no attempt to force his belief but whose every act of life was a setting forth of the facts which, to him, could not be denied. He answered every question of Frank Barnard's. One answer for instance: If two persons desire the same and only thing, the person with the most sincere desire will win. Victory comes to him who most desires it because he is, to the extent of his desire, willing to earn it.

"Then is it wholly a matter of desire and effort?"

"Not at all. There is also a mystery in accomplishment by Soul-desire which is beyond human understanding. This fact is positively and constantly proved by demonstration. The thing which CANNOT BE DONE *Is* DONE by Soul-desire or faith, if this term is more acceptable.

"Miracles are being performed daily by Soul-desire; individuals healing their own bodies and healing others by this God-given power. Hundreds of religious shrines all over the world testify to the presence and activity of this power today. The Indian "Medicine Man" of early America and the "Epileptic Shaman" of early history indicate the ever constant presence of this power with man.

"Happiness is one of the most easily obtained objectives. Material riches may be as readily secured but great

riches and happiness together form a combination difficult, indeed, to accomplish as you shall learn by my own
sad experience. Later, when you understand the meaning
of The Mark and the real reason of life, you will find it so
worth while the riches will be of far less importance."

IV

THE POWER OF
SOUL DESIRE

Let us now reason with the saying, 'When two or three are gathered together.' What can it mean other than, 'In unity there is strength'? Homer expresses it in six simple words, 'THE FORCE OF UNION CONQUERS ALL.'

"A united Soul-desire is an irresistible force. I will give you a simple business illustration. When a majority of souls in a city, state or country unite in the desire for good business conditions, the united soul of that city or country creates the belief of good business and to believe is to know. Therefore, when fifty-one per cent of the population know business is good, it IS GOOD. This is, indeed, a blunt simple statement. The refutation could be that business, in the ordinary course of events, happened to become good, and therefore, the majority knew it; but the explanation that things or conditions 'just happen' has no place in reasoning.

"Abraham Lincoln sought the aid of united Soul-desire during one of the darkest periods of the Civil War. He designated April 30th, 1863, as a day of confession and prayer, ending his proclamation with these words, 'All this being done in sincerity and truth, let us then rest humbly in the hope authorized by the divine teachings that the united cry of the nation will be heard on high, and answered with blessings no less than the pardon of our national sins and the restoration of our now divided and suffering country to its former happy condition of unity and peace.'

"Individual human selfishness is the great obstacle to united Soul-desire; but in times of calamity, quite frequently self is forgotten and God given a chance by the uniting of Soul-desire for the benefit of all.

"The stirring declaration of General Phillippe Petain, 'Ils ne passent pas' (They shall not pass) was so firmly imbedded in the souls of the French that it created a Soul-desire and a Soul-power which could not be overcome, regardless of the material odds against them. There were reports of angels with flaming swords and other supernatural occurrences which assisted the French in their heroic defense of Verdun; but, to my reasoning, the united Soul of France had the majority of power.

"It is a very common occurrence for small groups, an organization, for instance, to establish a united Soul-desire, which is clearly and positively manifested as the cause of the accomplishment.

"Seldom does this occur nationally and, more rarely, internationally; but fresh in your memory is an occurrence which, to me, was a vivid demonstration of international Soul-desire. What started this great united wave is not clear to me but you were one of the millions in this country whose inner self expressed a 'hope that he would make it.' You even *said* something like that. Millions in France said the same thing in another tongue; millions more in the British Isles and all over the civilized world had the hope and the desire for the success of one lone man. Thirty thousand fight fans in the Yankee Stadium, in New York, needed only a word from the veteran announcer, Joe Humphries, to be on their feet, bare-headed and united in silent prayer (soul-desire) that Lindbergh would reach the heart of France—a victor. It was later calculated that Lindbergh was at no time five miles off the direct course, when fifty miles would not have been considered much of a variance. Considering the limited equipment he had, does it not seem quite reasonable that there was some other guiding power, and can you conceive of any greater assistance than the united Soul-desire of the world? Perhaps you would like the wording better if I said, 'God, as He always has and always will, answered the united prayer of the majority of the people'; but I prefer to say, 'God's law operated, as it always has and always will.'

"Again I say, do not try to force yourself to believe this. Be satisfied with the thought that it could have happened in this way.

"Would there be need for Federal assistance provided a majority of souls desired a strict enforcement of the 18th Amendment? Of course not; because when a majority of souls desire a certain condition, it becomes a reality. When an individual has a Soul-desire, sincere enough to overcome any opposing desire, his sincere desire becomes a reality for him."

Such was the conception of God's law of Possession given to Frank Barnard by Paul Omar, the man who would give away millions, to change another man's price mark.

V

ONE OF THE GREAT COMMANDMENTS

The knowledge of this law of Possession had not come to Paul Omar suddenly but was revealed to him gradually through application combined with diligent study of cause and effect. With the unfolding of this great law came the intuitive warning of its danger. Possession would be a curse or a blessing depending upon its worth; and to choose wisely, he must solve the truth in values. His search for this knowledge over diversified paths seemed to end at a common center.

The Hebraic Law, a time-worn parchment, believed to have been inscribed 2500 years ago, reads, "Whatsoever you do not wish your neighbor to do to you, do not that to him," and added to it for emphasis, "This is the whole law. The rest is a mere exposition of it."

"The true rule of business is to guard and do by the things of others as they do by their own," was the way this law was written for the Hindu Kingdoms along the Ganges river 3500 years ago.

Later, in history, 1070 B. C., the Greeks knew of this law: "Do not that to thy neighbor which thee would take ill from him."

Was this, then, the "pearl of great price?" The sages of old seemed to think so but Omar could not find where it had been practised or given a fair trial.

That superwise Chinaman, Lao Tze, proclaimed it as follows: "Requite injury with kindness. To the not good I would be good in order to make them good."

At the first Buddistic Council, the Scribes advised: "One should seek for others the happiness one desires for one's self." In Persia: "Do as you would be done by." In the Koran of Mohammed is written: "Let none of you treat his brother in a way he himself would dislike to be treated." Confucius counsels: "What you would not wish done to yourself, do not unto others," and Moses said: "Thou shalt love thy neighbor as thyself."

This, then, was the conviction of the ages—the true value in life. This was the rule followed by his friend "Capital" that night in Seattle and Paul Omar resolved that his life would be dedicated to his fellow man. He would do unto others as had already been done unto him. The Golden Rule would be his guide and the Golden Square his symbol. Gold he would have, millions of it; not for himself but for the benefit of his brothers, the masses, who were in dense ignorance of God's law of Possession.

Humbly he would work with gratitude to God for enlightening him with the priceless knowledge that man may have his choice of destiny and that he has no enemy save that which is within himself.

VI

THE GOLDEN SQUARE
OF GOODWILL

The law of Possession worked perfectly. Wealth came in abundance and for quite a while his plan of establishing Philanthropic Funds was unnoticed; but as years went by, with interest earning interest, and thousands becoming millions, attention was attracted to Paul Omar.

This was not his wish. By word of mouth and in written statements to the press, he said so; but there was a slight satisfaction in seeing his picture on the front page and in hearing his modesty heralded as a virtue. A radical change was gradually coming over him. He began to welcome chances to talk about his great plans. His stationery was of the finest linen and graced with a small but attractive gold square.

One press notice referred to him as "Golden Square Omar." While he instructed his secretary to see that this did not happen again, he secretly liked it and indulged in several smug smiles of satisfaction. Small matters, these, but in his actual reasoning moments he knew they were not small, but of grave importance.

Man has no enemy except that which is within and Paul Omar knew the laws of his soul. Vanity is the parent demoralizer and Pride had taken root. He alone suspected it. He knew it and determined to weed it out; but Pride and Wealth are boon companions and a soul which has gratified all desires is weak; so his efforts were futile. He even boasted of reducing his resources by disbursing a greater percentage of his wealth; but this was not done. He also firmly resolved he would make no more speeches when his present engagements were filled but found himself weak again and booked for more far in advance. He was so busy that there was no time for, and little thought of, meditation. Conferences and interviews claimed him.

Plans were suggested for greater development of his present projects, plans for new endeavors; plans, plans, plans. Every one seemed to have a new one. All seemed good because he was being tactfully flattered.

Little by little suspicion seeped into his mind; first of one and then of another among those who sought his aid. Even his trusted confidential secretary was suspected of intrigue, and his good wife was regarded as a victim of imposition when she suggested a paltry five thousand donation to a neighborhood charity.

Full of self-pity and sick at heart, Paul Omar awoke to the fact that, with all his wealth, he was miserable. The rule that Gold and Happiness are seldom congenial comrades had proved true, even to him, with all his knowledge. The trouble was, he was full of pride. "What a fool I have been," he told himself, "to let it grow, but now I will root it out. . . . I still have my *will* power."

VII

THE INCOMPETENCY
OF WILL POWER

*"There is no passion which steals into the heart more
imperceptibly and covers itself under more disguises
than Pride."*

—ADDISON.

All engagements were cancelled and the word was
passed that Paul Omar was going to England but,
instead, he made entirely different arrangements. Dressed
in an old suit, he boarded a night train for Seattle. Meals
were served in his drawing room. He let his beard grow
to further his disguse. Only twice did he leave the train;
once at Pocatello, where there was quite a stop, and again
at Portland the next afternoon, where he was forced to
change Pullmans on account of a hot box.

Arriving after dark at Seattle, he registered at the old
Washington Hotel as "William Jones of Los Angeles" and

felt quite safe from recognition. For two days he wandered through streets so familiar to him in his boy-hood, around the docks and through the stores. He passed the place where he lived as a boy but the old frame building was gone and a three-story brick tenement stood in its place. No one knew him. It made him lonesome. He wanted to talk to some one; so he went out to the ship-yards. Bill Oleman, now boss of the yards, recognized him at once and Paul Omar was delighted. He wanted to be recognized. The fact that he shaved before starting out indicated it. What a reception the boys gave him! Of course, the news flashed through the city. His picture, with the story of his early life and rise to wealth, occupied the front page of the Daily Times next morning. Such a story it was! . . . "Golden Square Omar, the nationally-known philanthropist, who once was Seattle's orphan waif, without a chance . . . now back home with power to give *all* a chance."

There was no avoiding publicity after that article. Explanations of his Funding Plans were in demand and requests for contributions came pouring in. He was back in the lime-light and doing a great worthy work. . . . Paul Omar, the man among men, with confidence in himself and these good Western people, was talking "self" again, with a new vigor but still the wrong viewpoint: HIS was the power, not GOD's.

On the last day of the week, among the many callers waiting to have a word with him was one who appeared to be a substantial, conservative, well-balanced business man, quite likely a banker. He was slight of build, with sparce gray hair, rather heavy brows and a face that impelled confidence. His attitude of tranquility, when a late comer of self-importance rudely pushed by him, was noticed by Omar, who smilingly gave him recognition. Mr. Omar was surprised to learn that he was the Reverend George Brown, pastor of the wealthiest church in Seattle.

His mission was not one of money but a request for moral assistance. He would be grateful, his wealthy congregation would be helped, the poor of Seattle would profit and God would be pleased if Paul Omar would talk in his church at the eleven o'clock service the following day. The subject, of course, would be his experiences and joys in the application of the Golden Rule.

The invitation was accepted, but George Brown, Priest of God, walked down crowded Second Avenue that Saturday morning much perplexed. Had he acted wisely? What would his followers—those well-to-do, complacent men and women—think of it? Would he be criticized for inviting a Jew to occupy the chancel and talk to those who professed the Christian faith? . . . A prayer flashed out of his soul. The answer came, immediately, direct and positive: "Peace be unto you. It is My will."

How true it is, "God moves in a mysterious way, His wonders to perform."

VIII

THE NEW VISION

Sunday was one of those perfect days so common in Seattle. The air was just crisp and salt enough to encourage physical exercise. Paul Omar never felt more fit as he walked from his hotel to the foot of James Street and, although the cable car was about to start up the hill, he decided to walk the rest of the way to the ivy-covered church where he was to tell Seattle's Best of his experiences. This he would do with extreme modesty, so he told himself, but the tall hat and new frock coat he had just purchased seemed a little contradictory to a humble demeanor.

At the church, the Reverend Mr. Brown gave him a cordial welcome, explained the order of the service in which he was to have an important part, and hurt his feelings, somewhat, when he designated the top step of the chancel where he was to stand when making the address. In Omar's opinion, the beautifully carved pulpit would have been more fitting; but, apparently, it was not customary.

Seated alone in the front center pew of the large, well-filled church, he listened with interested admiration to the sincerity of the priest and was impressed with the solemnity of the service. Kneeling and standing with the congregation, he endeavored to get the meaning of their responses and prayers. Long ago, at college, he had studied this service but, today, one line of the Creed seemed strangely significant to him: "I believe in the Holy Ghost, the Lord and giver of life." He recalled once consulting the Americana for the definition of Holy Spirit and finding three words "See Holy Ghost." . . . Strange this thought should come to him now but it was dismissed instantly as all arose to sing the hymn which preceded his talk.

Paul Omar had the correct place in the Hymnal, number 289, but he was so deeply engrossed with the opening remarks of his talk that he neither saw the words nor heard the tune. It ended with a glorious "Amen," and his time to speak had come.

With dignity he stepped out of the pew and took his

place, the book still in his hand and his first finger marking the hymn just sung.

Firmly he expostulated, counselled and recommended The Golden Rule, from every angle. He was sincere and impressive, although a wee bit too loud of voice for this sacred place. The address ended with these words: "If you will live on the square and follow the Golden Rule, life will have full meaning for you."

IX

THE POWER OF THAT STILL SMALL VOICE OF CONSCIENCE

He took his seat, finger still dividing the pages of the book, and the service continued with a solemnity in such contrast with his speech that the hot blood rose in his veins. . . . He laid the book down, open at the place his finger had marked and mopped the perspiration from his face and neck. . . . If he could only get out in the cool air he would feel better—but that front pew was *such* a long distance from the door! And although he looked around several times, once even starting to go, he finally decided it could not be done without discourtesy; so he would stick it out. . . . "I believe in the Holy Ghost" flashed again through his mind. . . . What a fool he had been—boasting of *his* plan in God's house, even though it was not of his faith. . . .

Quite a majority of the congregation were devoutly going to the altar. He knew it was the Communion. Some people had queer ideas as to the Holy Presence at this service. . . .

. . . The atmosphere became suffocating! His head seemed in a whirl! What he wanted was to *get out* and not attract attention. Restlessly twisting around, his body touched the book still open and he picked it up. . . .

"The Body of our Lord Jesus Christ which was given for thee

The Blood of our Lord, Jesus Christ, which was shed for thee"

came softly to his ears as he read the hymn:

"Come, Holy Ghost our souls inspire,
And lighten with celestial fire.
Thou the anointing Spirit art,
Who dost Thy sevenfold gifts impart.

Thy blessed unction from above
Is comfort, life, and fire of love.
Enable with perpetual light
The dullness of our blinded sight.

Anoint and cheer our soiled face
With the abundance of Thy grace.
Keep far our foes, give peace at home:
Where Thou art guide, no ill can come.

Teach us to know the Father, Son,
And Thee of both to be but one,
That through the ages all along,
This may be our endless song:

Praise to Thy eternal merit,
Father, Son, and Holy Spirit."

With the last line he laid, or rather dropped, the book on the seat beside him, and the church seemed to swim. . . . How brilliantly the Cross shone through the blur! . . . What were they singing? Who *was* it singing? There were no words, and yet, there *must* have been, because he heard, distinctly, above the song, his name, his name in the song. . . . "Lo, this is the man that made not God his strength, but trusted in the abundance of his riches and strengthened himself in his wickedness." . . . "O God! Grant me Peace." . . . "Paul!" . . . "Master, what wouldest Thou?" . . . "Knowest not that I gave thee *all?"*. . . "Yea, Lord, whosoever Thou art, forgive, forgive."

"I am the Holy Comforter, sent by the love of Jesus Christ, Son of the Eternal God, to heal your tortured soul. Look to the CROSS, glorify God in the highest, and receive the wisdom and peace thou seekest.. . . No earnest prayer remains unanswered. Thinkest thou the law of majority is for this small world—alone? Thinkest thou there is no higher form of thinking life than pigmy man? Thou hast been blind, indeed. . . . Canst thou not read the answer to that earnest suppliant cry of the majority of ages past; that overwhelming desire for God to come to this earth?: 'THERE WAS A SONG IN THE NIGHT, A GREAT STAR'S LIGHT AND THE FACE OF A CHILD DIVINE.'

"That was the answer, Paul, to the majority of Soul-desire at the beginning of your present calendar for recording time. God came to this earth, incarnate in Jesus, child of Nazareth; lived a perfect human life of love as an example for all; demonstrated the power of faith and its effect on material things; shared human suffering and temptations; died on the cross and demonstrated the power of faith in the spiritual world by His resurrection and reappearance.

"Your Golden Square, symbol of the Golden Rule,

represents only the *material* life, which so soon passes away. The Kingdom of God is ETERNAL. The Cross of Christ Jesus, one with the Father, is a symbol on your earth for the *first* and *great commandment:* 'Thou shalt love the Lord thy God with all thy heart and with all thy soul and with all thy mind.' Love and glorify God Eternal, Who was and is and always will be. PERFECT PEACE, which you so much desire, is impossible without faith in Eternal God and in the eternal life of your spirit.

"Continue your earthly progress with the full knowledge that your place in the eternal home of God will be as near to Him as you are able to prepare for it during your human life.

"Follow the example of Christ Jesus. Disregard not your symbol of the Golden Square, but, to the glory of God, put the cross of Christ ABOVE it."

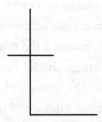

Indistinctly he could see the Cross on the altar shining through the fog. . . . "And the Blessing of God Almighty, the Father, the Son and the Holy Ghost be amongst you and remain with you always. Amen."

"Onward Christian Soldiers, marching as to war,
With the cross of Jesus going on before."

They were marching out. The Reverend Mr. Brown touched him as he passed and whispered, "Wait for me."

Paul Omar was *alive*, dazed a little, but with a peace of soul beyond understanding. The Holy Presence was now a *reality* to him. A gentleman came from across the aisle, saying, "Sorry, sir, your time was limited. I should have liked so much to hear more, particularly regarding the spiritual satisfaction you must enjoy."

"I, too, am sorry I could not have told about that," replied Omar, in a voice he hardly recognized as his own; a new voice, quite low, but filled with a peculiar magnetic quality of sureness, peace and love.

Together they walked to the door—the last to leave; and as the hand of George Brown clasped that of Paul Omar, there was a bond of understanding which no words can describe. Each knew that both were at peace—that peace which passeth human understanding and comes to so few, and *only* comes from a positive conviction of Eternal Life and Life Immortal.

Five days later, Omar was home again—a new man with a new price mark symbolic of his earthly requirements, his reason for life and, above all, a constant declaration of Life Eternal. The Cross of Christ, representing the first and great Commandment; the square of humanity, representing the second; blended together in the mysterious symbol on and through which Paul Omar has built his life, his fortune and his happiness.

Naturally, hearing the brief outline of Omar's life and knowing the general meaning of his price mark on unlimited wealth and happiness, was to Barnard only the *beginning* of his education in a philosophy which would bring to *him* the same result if he could understand and practice it; so their enjoyable evenings together continued and still continue to this day.

Barnard, guided by the Cross and the Square, is becoming an outstanding success in his long-hoped-for secret ambition to be a great artist. Money has little place in his life but comes easily and in large amounts.

Paul Omar, that modest, powerful personality, is daily living his interpretation of God's desire for the unity of love as demonstrated by the person and life of the Man of Galilee. His continued contributions in millions amaze the world; yet little, if any, thought is given to his far greater asset—the working knowledge of God's laws.

So endeth the story of the Meaning of the Mark.

But knowing that you, dear reader, are hungry for more facts and have many questions you would like answered, an attempt is made to satisfy this longing by a second version of the Meaning of the Mark, explaining the philosophy of Paul Omar, his rules of accomplishment, the reason for them and some definite facts and experiences of others who have proved the never-failing laws with results so mystifying that they defy all reasoning.

VERSION

II

X

THE "HOW" OF PAUL OMAR'S PHILOSOPHY

Man is an Organ of Life and God alone is life.
—SWEDENBORG.

The philosophy of Paul Omar teaches that the Kingdom of God is LIFE—on this earth—right now, and that man has been given the power to become the most important factor in it. The requirements necessary to harness this power, however, baffle accomplishment by their extreme simplicity.

Man, in his worldly wisdom, is using less than one per cent of his God-given power of achievement.

"Seek ye first the Kingdom of God and His righteousness," as interpreted by Omar, means to accept the bounteous gifts of wealth, health, happiness and understanding offered by God in return for your expressing His purpose on this earth.

God's apparent purpose for man's life on earth is progress toward a life of individual and united love, which means a harmonious existence, one with another, brought about by the understanding and operation of His fixed laws.

Merely giving you the simple rules to accomplishment, with brief instructions as to their use*, while beneficial, is not satisfying. You want to know the reason back of the rule and, therefore, we must start with the fundamentals, the laws and explanations of them, so that you may use this knowledge to offset the false conception you may now have.

---

* This is available in the book "It Works."

XI

THE THREE FUNDAMENTALS

First Fundamental—

The first fundamental is that man has a mind, objective in character, being the function of a physical brain. It is the outgrowth of man's physical necessities and its normal method of observation is through the five physical senses.

It is man's material and physical guide. Its highest function is that of reasoning by inductive, deductive, analytic and synthetic methods.

The mind of man, while possessing no powers whatever independent of physical organization, directs man's destiny.

It has, in general, little or no faith beyond objective reason.

The mind of man, under normal conditions, is not controllable against his will, his reason, his positive knowledge or the evidence of his senses by the minds or suggestion of another.

For our purpose, let us define inductive reasoning as starting from certain particular facts rather than from a general law. The propositions derived from inductive reasoning do not cover every single case of the law it endeavors to establish. Inductive reasoning accepts as truth a theory which cannot be proved except by results. Inductive reasoning starts with a theory to fit the facts, then proceeds to verify the results, observing errors and, if necessary, formulates a new theory, on the basis of observed data, avoiding the errors.

The necessity for inductive reasoning is lack of knowledge concerning the central fact or concerning the law governing the facts.

Second Fundamental—

The second fundamental is that man has a soul which is a distinct entity possessing independent powers and functions.

The soul has a mental organization of its own and is capable of sustaining an existence independently of the body.

It is the substance, essence and expression of faith, possessing a dynamic force independent of body, CAPABLE OF ANY ACCOMPLISHMENT.

It is the seat of all emotions and is in constant, absolute control of every function, condition and sensation of the body.

It is the storehouse of memory and never discards any thought or action of the mind.

The soul can and does communicate with the souls of other persons. This faculty is unlimited by time and space.

It communicates with the mind intuitively.

Knowing all of nature's (God's) laws, the soul has no need for, and is incapable of, inductive reasoning but is all capable of deductive reasoning.

Its one limitation is inability to formulate its own premises. (This means that the soul can start no activity without instruction from the mind to do so.)

THIRD FUNDAMENTAL—

The third fundamental is that suggestion is the all potent factor of both soul and mind.

The soul of man is unqualifiedly and constantly amenable to the mind of man and the power of suggestion.

Suggestions from the mind—often registered uncon-sciously—are constantly guiding and controlling the functions of the soul.

The soul of a man is more amenable to the suggestions of his own mind than to suggestions from the mind of another.

The control of soul by mind—which is mortal and physical—makes man a free moral agent with the power to train or direct his soul for weal or woe.

There you have the three fundamentals of Omar's philoso-phy boiled down for the purpose in mind; namely, understand-ing a simple method that will give you any and every thing you want. You do not necessarily have to believe this statement to accomplish the result.

XII

RIGHT THINKING NECESSARY

How can I get what I want, whether or not it is good for me to have it? I'll take the chance. Give me that million," is about the verbal expression of the non-thinking human being; and to the outburst might well be added, "How can I get it for nothing and keep everyone else from having it?"

The philosophy being explained to you assumes to do that very thing, provided it is your wish. You are promised anything you want, if you can follow the right path.

Later on, you will be given three laws, which work as positively as all laws of nature, but for the present we will analyze the three fundamentals.

Briefly, the fundamentals state that while your soul has ultimate control of every happening in your life, nevertheless, your soul has no self-starter. Mind, alone, does the starting; your mind or another's. In other words, your soul is constantly directing your body in its functions, telling each atom what to do. Therefore, if your mind is telling or suggesting to your soul to do something which your reason says is not good for you, naturally you are getting what you direct and are causing the thing not good for you to happen. *It is very important that this situation be thoroughly understood.*

You may not want something to happen but if you fear it, naturally you are thinking about it and the soul acts on this thought. You are making your own conditions by your thoughts.

Faith is the essential prerequisite to the successful exercise of power.

Christ, when living on this earth in the man Jesus, being limited by God's laws for mortals, did not hesitate to acknowledge his inability to heal the sick in the absence of faith. Just why faith is necessary can not be answered but it is known and proved to be a fact.

This statement need not be discouraging to you, as the first fundamental states that the mind has no faith beyond objective reasoning; while the second says the soul is the substance and essence of faith; and the third fundamental explains that soul acts at the suggestion of the mind. It has no alternative. *Therefore, it is not necessary that the mind believe the suggestion possible of accomplishment in order for the soul to obtain the result.*

After results have been accomplished time upon time and the mind knows, by objective results, that the system operates without fail, then the mind also acquires faith. AT THIS STAGE, NOTHING IS IMPOSSIBLE.

For sake of emphasis, the faith required may be purely soul faith, and the requirement to soul-action sincere mental desire, communicated by suggestion—not retarded by abnormal active opposition in the way of adverse suggestion from the mind.

XIII

THE FAMOUS LITTLE RED BOOK "IT WORKS"

Well, what about that million you want; or the new car; or many other material things of little value? Can they be obtained by just thinking about them? Yes indeed; unqualifiedly, according to this philosophy; but, do you really think about what you want or are you most of the time thinking and talking about what you do not want? Be fair with yourself in answering this question. Isn't it a fact that you are today getting just the things about which you think most? Wasn't today about what you expected it would be?

The brain functions rather arbitrarily most of the time. The mind has thousands of thoughts in the course of an hour. The soul records them all and acts on the dominant thought. The most powerful and constant suggestion receives first attention.

There is found, in the book "It Works," a definite plan for soul communication. It reads as follows:

"Write down on paper in order of their importance the things and conditions you really want.

"Do not be afraid of wanting too much. Go the limit in writing down your wants.

"Change the list daily, adding to or taking from it until you have it about right. Do not be discouraged on account of changes, as this is natural.

"There will always be changes and additions with accomplishments and increasing desires.

Three Positive Rules to Accomplishment:

Rule 1. Read the list of what you want three times each day—morning, noon and night.

Rule 2. Think of what you want as often as possible.

Rule 3. Do not talk to any one about your plan except to the Great Power within you which will unfold to your mind the method of accomplishment."

XIV

THE LAW OF "COMEBACK"

✶

It would be hard to give a more concrete or more definite plan for suggesting to the soul or for getting what you want; but have a care! Nothing, so far, has been said about the three laws, the first of which is:

LAW ONE
"As ye sow, so shall ye reap."

"Give, and it shall be given unto you; good measure, pressed down, and shaken together, and running over, shall men give into your bosom. For with the same measure that ye mete withal it shall be measured to you again" (Luke 6:38). You have heard this law quoted in many ways and up to the present it probably has meant little to you. BE ASSURED THAT IT OPERATES WITH EXCEEDING ACCURACY AT ALL TIMES.

"This law is called 'The Law of Karma,' meaning 'comeback.' Man receives only that which he gives. The game of life is a game of boomerangs: man's thoughts, deeds and words returning to him sooner or later with astounding accuracy." Often this is not in the nature of a desire for something.

John and Bill were bosom friends living in different cities. John had an ideal home life; while Bill, at least in John's opinion, had a "millstone around his neck" in the shape of an indolent, lazy wife.

John arrived in Bill's town one Saturday morning. Bill took John home to dinner. Mrs. Bill knew he was coming but when they arrived there was a lack of welcome—no indication of any preparation for dinner. Mrs. Bill was sitting in the living room complaining of the heat and suggested dinner at some convenient restaurant.

Bill was somewhat upset but turned in with a wonderful show of good humor, got the dinner as though he were accustomed to it, and everything went off smoothly with the exception of John's increasing disgust for Mrs. Bill. He even told Bill what he thought but Bill only laughed it off.

John proceeded on his way and for the next few years the principal topic of his conversation was: "Poor Bill and his lazy wife." It took him just about three years to wake up to the fact that his own wife had changed and was about as useless to him as any wife could be.

Some five years later Bill took a trip with his family and called on John. What he thought of Mrs. John is not known, but John noticed that Mrs. Bill was not half bad; in fact, he wished his wife were as companionable. Later, some one sent John that little red book "It Works." This started him in the study of correcting his condition.

Both Mrs. John and Mrs. Bill are living ideally today, but the point is this: John, by his constant dwelling on Bill's lazy wife offered this suggestion to his soul and received what he most thought of and least wanted: a lazy wife of his own.

The story of Bill and John is true and illustrates the effect of the mind on the soul and the power of the soul to bring about the reality of a thought. You may say "it just happened"; but when thousands of such events happen in the same way, it ceases to be coincidental. John was sowing a "crop of lazy wives" and the harvest could not have been otherwise. Had he, regardless of his opinion, expended the same time, attention and remarks to the charming qualities of Mrs. Bill, his wife, as well as Bill's, would have been what he helped to make them—industrious and charming.

Nothing "just happens." There is a reason for every result. There is a cause for every effect.

Do you think it was a coincidence that all those sages of old expressed in one way or another what we know as the Golden Rule: "Do unto others as you would they should do unto you"? Why should they recommend such a procedure if it were not profitable? Does not this really imply: you may expect others to treat you as you treat them; or, "whatsoever a man soweth, that shall he also reap"? Would you like to prove it this day? Well, start out with love in your heart for every human being alive and you will receive love in return today. Hate—and hate will return to you. Cheat—and you will be cheated. Give—and you will receive. Hold back—and it shall be held back from you.

There is no evading this law and it goes further. If you secure something through your soul power and, by so doing, injure another, you will pay in full—no more, no less—in the same mysterious way you received and injured. That is the way Law Number One operates and, because of the observation of this law, the Golden Rule was recommended and even explained as the summary of the law by the Hebrews of old.

Is it wisdom or ignorance to disregard such a law when we see it in daily operation? Pause and think this over because you are going to prove the power of the soul to give you what you want by actual results and it is of vital importance that you use this power wisely. You may be ever so wise but you can not change the Law of Compensation. You will receive in proportion to what you give—measure for measure. That is God's law, a gift to you and all mankind.

There are enough riches in the world to make every man a millionaire without injury to another. There is also a plentiful supply of poverty for all who desire it; but it is rather difficult to acquire without injury to yourself and others.

Mrs. Annabell Grayson was not her name but she was 62 years old and the wife of a minister. Her husband, the Rev. Mr. Grayson, died in 1927, leaving an estate of some $5500, $3500 of which was represented by a certificate of stock in a well-known automobile company headed by an aviation ace. Just how this stock was acquired is not known but the company was in the hands of a receiver at the time of Mr. Grayson's death. The stock was worth not more than ten cents on the dollar and could not be sold for five.

Mrs. Grayson interviewed an attorney who, for the sum of twenty-five dollars, investigated her chances and informed her that the stock was valueless. Then some one sent her the book "It Works," containing the plan and rules you have read. Probably Mrs. Grayson was not so well informed in business matters but she, at least, was sensible enough to take a chance, as it cost nothing. She wrote down that she wanted instructions in converting the certificate for $3500 into real money. In less than a week, she had convinced herself that the Rev. Alward Jones—and this is not his name—of Indianapolis, who went through the seminary at Greensburg with her husband, would help her. (Her soul could and probably did tell her this.) So she went to Indianapolis and put the problem before him. He was helpless, having had no experience in the investment field but suggested their calling on Franklin Wills (not his name), president of an automobile manufacturing company, who was one of his parishioners.

Wills listened to the story, looked at the certificate and then at the little gray-haired lady so sweet in her simplicity, saying, "Mother, the lawyer who told you this stock was no good did not know his business. I will cash it for you. Take this check of mine to the Union Trust Company, sign your name on the back and they will give you the $3500; and when you get home tell that lawyer to give you back your twenty-five dollars, because he erred."

Just another coincidence, was it? The stock is not now worth ten cents on the dollar but that automobile manufacturer followed a hunch—which came to him shortly after this occurrence—to lower the price on his line of cars and to do another more radical and apparently unreasonable thing in connection with his marketing.

As Mrs. Grayson's gain—brought about by him—took her estate from the debit to the credit side of her ledger, so did the changes in price and method put that automobile company on a handsome profit basis the following year. Another "coincidence" brought about by sowing the right kind of seed and reaping a full, rich harvest.

Mrs. Grayson told her part of this story. A news item in an automotive magazine furnished the data for the finish.

Do not let fear of the action of the Karmic law keep you from using your soul power to gain any possession that may be of benefit to yourself or others. In most cases your common sense is a safe guide. If there is doubt in your mind that you may be injuring others, make your request or petition conditional upon the general welfare and God's approval. Cast on Him the burden of the decision and its results.

Your soul will answer you intuitively. You also have the Ten Commandments and the Golden Rule to guide you. Anything not in violation of these three guides for human action—which have stood the test of time—is good for you to have: Riches, Health, Happiness and Love.

Proceed according to the plan and follow the three rules taken from "It Works":—

Write down what you want.

Keep it in your mind constantly.

Figure out how you might possibly get it. Affirm it is already yours in the idea and you have by this action of the mind planted the seed in the soul. You have started something and if you will nourish it by continued affirmation and act upon the intuitive message from your soul, you will accomplish your desire.

Your soul may tell you to work for it along certain lines or it may come to you in the way of a coincidence—so-called; but remember, when it comes—no matter in what way—give thanks to God for giving you a soul power capable of the accomplishment.

In other words, thank your soul, whether or not your mind believes your soul had anything to do with the result. If you do this, your mind will finally have faith and then, with the combined faith of soul and mind, you can accomplish the impossible.

If, on the other hand, you consider your accomplishment a coincidence and make this affirmation or attribute the result to your own natural-born cleverness, you will not encourage belief in or use of your soul power consciously or intelligently.

Mary Humphrey is private secretary to the president of a large hardware manufacturing concern. She received "It Works." The plan sounded foolish but she thought it worth a trial, so she wrote down that she wanted a diamond ring. Then she followed the details of selecting the ring, wrote down the jeweler's name, the price of the ring, the setting chosen, and diligently read what she had written for four days; but nothing happened. She decided it was all "hooey," to use her term, and told her employer about the silly book. He read it and told her it was the finest plan for accomplishment he knew, incidentally inquiring if she had tried it. "Yes," replied Mary, "but it didn't work."

This was in October. On the 25th of December of that year Mr. and Mrs. Employer gave Mary the identical ring she had selected. Just how he found the slip with the written desire and description of the ring is not known; but

Mary is still telling of the remarkable "coincidence" and the poor, overly-wise girl who performed this simple accomplishment by soul power is still in ignorance of her power of possession. Her total result was just one ring ahead, which is really pathetic.

Here is another "ring" incident:—

Rose Marie is an employee at a beauty parlor in Chicago. Weekly she did the hair of Mrs. Gaylord. One day she related to her customer how she had paid a dollar a week on a ring in a jewelry club. Each week she was told that she would win and assured that no one could contribute fifty weeks without winning. She won—after depositing forty-five dollars but, upon having the ring appraised, she found it worth about two dollars.

Now forty-five dollars was a fortune to Rose Marie and Mrs. Gaylord was much concerned. She took the matter up with Mr. Gaylord who that day had read "It Works." He suggested that she write down her desires; so she wrote "I want Rose Marie to get back her forty-five dollars" and she diligently followed directions; but nothing happened for many days. Still she persevered.

After two weeks time Mr. Gaylord interested himself in the matter. He called on the Police Department but did not get very far. Several days later he called on the Vice President of a leading Chicago newspaper, who gave him a letter to a police official. Then action started. A plain-clothes man, accompanied by Mr. Gaylord, called at the office of the jewelry club where the money was refunded. That night Mr. Gaylord said to his wife. "You may scratch off that one want from your list. Here is Rose Marie's forty-five dollars."

Call this "coincidence" but if the plan had not been followed or if Mr. Gaylord had never heard of it through the book, Rose Marie would never have recovered her money.

These true stories are told to encourage and persuade you consciously to direct your soul power. When you fail to do so consciously, rest assured you do so unconsciously— usually to your detriment.

You may get some consolation out of alibis for your condition in life; but after reading the plan, the rules and the experiences of others, there is certainly no excuse for at least not trying to demonstrate God's great gift—your soul power for achievement.

"The vision that you glorify in your mind, the ideal that you enthrone in your heart, this you will build your life by, this you will become."

—James Allen.

"A desire in the heart for anything is God's sure promise sent beforehand to indicate that it is yours already in the limitless realm of supply."

—H. Emilie Cady.

XV

SILENCE FOSTERS FAITH

Rule Three in "It Works" tells you not to talk of your plan or the result of your experiments with soul power. The reason is two-fold. If you have been unsuccessful, most of your listeners will agree with you that the plan is foolish. If successful and you tell about it, they will doubt you; and unless you have a firm conviction of this truth you may lose the faith you have gained.

Billy Hoyne was cross-eyed. A Christian Science practitioner, after several treatments, succeeded in straightening the eye. Billy knew it was straight. He saw it in the practitioner's mirror and was very happy. Just outside he met a friend and said to him, "Look! Chistian Science straightened my eye!" The friend did not believe in Christian Science and his face expressed his disbelief as he looked at Billy's eye. The doubt was communicated to Billy by telepathy: "You're crazy!" was about the substance of the message; and he looked into the show window of Marshall Field's to convince himself it was still straight. The result could not have been otherwise—he was afraid the eye might have gone crooked again and—it had!

This story came direct from Billy to his employer. His eye was straightened again by the same practitioner, but not until six months later.

While this is a tribute to Christian Science, and many remarkable accomplishments are performed in that faith, any one of a dozen other methods would have gotten the same result—to be as easily reversed as this one was that day when Billy inadvisedly talked to his doubting friend and then looked into the window. This is a true story and a good illustration of why you should not talk of your power of possession until you have a conviction which cannot be shaken or changed.

John Weitzel was a day laborer. His wife, Helen, did odd jobs to increase the family income. They promised themselves that Anna, their three-year-old daughter, would have an education and advantages denied them. Then a second daughter, Mary, was born. The doctor said she was blind.

Helen Weitzel, strong in her Catholic faith, took her problem to God. She did not question the cause of this tragedy. She only wanted relief from it—the child's eyesight restored. Her only hope sprang from simple faith in a healing shrine. She knew that thousands were healed each year at Ste. Anne de Beaupré; so she decided to take the baby there.

John was not in favor of her spending their money to do so. He reasoned if the doctors could not help Mary, there was no hope; but Helen, braving the harshness of her husband, with undaunted courage, took the family savings for the trip. At Ste. Anne, she went up the steps on her knees, a prayer on every step; but no miracle happened!

Home she came, still strong in her faith. She had seen others healed and reasoned that her prayers were not correctly said. Perhaps, because of John's attitude, they were not. Immediately she went to work as a scrub woman, at night, to earn the money for another trip. Two years later, she made a second pilgrimage. Again she went up the steps, again she prayed and, again nothing happened.

Home again. She once more began to work and save for the third journey. Two years passed, years of toil and undaunted faith. When Mary was five years old, this courageous mother again took her child to the healing shrine. Half way up the long flight of steps the miracle happened. The eyes of the child were opened! Helen's great faith had won.

No one can tell Helen Weitzel that God did not do this and she is right. She worked His law correctly. There was no interference from John the third time. Her overtowering faith had surmounted every obstacle.

The doctors might claim that some dirt or grit in the child's eyes had cut the film which covered the pupils. Could Helen believe this? Would she say it "just happened"?

Mary is now 24 years old and a private secretary with a beautiful pair of strong blue eyes. She wears no glasses. Anne, her sister, a brilliant business woman, told me this story. It is repeated to you to illustrate the effect of soul power.

XVI

GREAT SOULS RELY
ON GOD

What difference does it make what method is used if the result is secured.

Ste. Anne de Beaupré and those God-fearing priests of old who started this healing shrine have relieved thousands upon thousands of suffering humanity; and if your soul suggests a visit to Ste. Anne, obey the suggestion; if to Christian Science or your physician, follow the suggestion.

It may be true, and doubtless is, that one great source of the power of drugs to heal disease is attributable to the suggestion of the mind to the soul of the patient at the time the drug is administered. This being true, it follows that when a patient believes in drugs, drugs should be administered.

Anything within or without reason you can do to make the mind behave as you wish, should be done. Whether the found horse-shoe be nailed "toes up or toes down" makes little difference if the result is obtained. Many a horse chestnut carried in the left trouser pocket has cured rheumatism of long standing and the bones of many people always ache just before a storm. We laugh at the absurdity of the old Indian medicine man, who painted his face so grotesquely and waved frantically a highly-colored bladder while performing his cure; but his methods worked. Today, for mental effect, we often find a beautiful bouquet of American Beauties in the operating room of the mental healer.

The mind of man is swayed in numerous ways and "fortunate indeed is he who has found the key to the control of his mind"; or, in other words, fortunate indeed is he who has learned how to pray so that his prayers are answered.

An outstanding personality in Chicago, Father David Gibson, head of the Cathedral Shelter (Episcopal) at Peoria Street and Washington Boulevard, is such a man. At the Shelter, the bread line of unfortunates at times seems to be without end. Food, clothing and shoes must be had in enormous quantities but all are fed and clothed and comforted. When Father Gibson is out of shoes, he prays for shoes—and gets them. His needs are supplied—his prayers are answered. The same prayers said, with the same vocal expression, before the same altar, by some one else, might bring no result. The difference is simply this: Father Gibson knows that he will get the shoes or anything else needed. He puts the situation up to God—and the shoes, or whatever else it is, arrive. The average mind is sure such a procedure could not possibly be reasonable and, of course, to such a mind it is not.

To make the mind behave as you wish it to, or to have your prayers answered, is not an easy matter—even after you have actually proved this can be accomplished; and if any material object: the crucifix, a holy shrine, a bouquet of flowers, the sea, a mountain peak, a dose of medicine, or a painted bladder, will assist you, by all means use it.

XVII

AS A MAN THINKETH, SO IS HE

In a small Ohio town lives an inventor whose name is known over the world. He has studied and understands most of the systems of accomplishment by so-called "Mind over Matter" methods. He has proved, beyond any doubt, that he can, by faith of his mind and soul, accomplish results apparently impossible to all material and scientific laws.

He lives in a beautiful country house, surrounded by his birds, flowers and dumb animal friends, demonstrating with them and obtaining results which, if told, would detract from, rather than add to, the object of this book. They are unreasonable, apparently unreal, and cannot be believed by others even when actually proved by the senses of sight and hearing.

You would presume, then, that such a man, having demonstrated the power of God capable of such miracles, would have the ability to control his mind under all conditions; but such is not the case.

Many years ago he was afflicted with what physicians termed "weak valvular control." The valves of the heart and other organs fail to function at certain times, causing collapse. These collapses usually occur when he is in the company of acquaintances who know of his affliction and who are momentarily expecting a collapse. The mind of the acquaintance apparently communicates to him by telepathy, the valves cease to work, and down he goes—usually at a most embarrassing moment or in the most inconvenient place.

Proof that such collapses are controllable by the mind was unquestionably demonstrated by the writer this last summer. The inventor was showing me his new car, driving at the rate of sixty or more miles per hour with perfect control; but upon alighting at the far end of his estate to issue instructions to some of his workmen, the "valve thought" took possession of him and he started to sway. In less than two seconds I had a cigar in my mouth, felt for a match and said loudly, "Darn the luck, I haven't a match! Have you one?" The effect was instantaneous. His hand went to his vest pocket for a match;

the "valve thought" was arrested and the body became normal.

The inventor knew he was "going"; he knew why he snapped out of it. When I suggested that I drive the car home, he said: "Don't be afraid. I never have any trouble when I am driving. That is why I drive so fast—I can't think of anything except controlling the car." In other words, the valve trouble came only when he thought of it.

There are two reasons for this illustration. First, to show the difficulty of erasing a wrong idea that has become established in the mind—a difficulty justifying the use of suggestion supplied by a material object or otherwise. Second, that when this inventor friend of mine reads his own case, he may be awakened to see the foolishness of this situation and to find the method of forcing his mind to continually suggest a perfect physical organism.

XVIII

A PROVEN PLAN OF ACCOMPLISHMENT

In the plan copied from "It Works," the material object suggested as an assistance in directing the mind is your written list of what you want, definitely described in detail—

If money, the amount you want and how you might
get it.
If an automobile, the make, color, price and where
sold.
If a trip, where, when and with whom.

You are told to make a written list because your vacillating mind is prone to forget. You read your list three times a day to fix it firmly in your mind; and you talk of your plan to no one, lest they may weaken your faith by wrong suggestion.

As long as you live, your soul is constantly acting upon the suggestions that are dominant in your mind.

You must realize that on yourself alone rests the responsibility of directing your life and fortune. Hence you must correctly and intelligently govern your mind's action at all times.

You were told that the requirements were so simple that you might overlook them and you, time upon time, have agreed with the saying: "As a man thinketh, so is he"; but it should mean more to you now, inasmuch as you must understand the importance of consciously directing your thought.

What about the million?

Are you still thinking it is not for you?

Possibly "One Hundred Thousand" is all your vision can encompass.

Whether it is to be a five-dollar increase in the weekly pay envelope or the blue slip of dismissal; whether it is to be the announcement that you have been appointed to control, or reduced to the ranks; whether you are to be one of the four hundred or one of the four million—is Up TO YOU PERSONALLY.

If you really want to accomplish something, you must

START. Lay out your plan and follow it. Nothing of importance occurs without a plan; and one sure way to check up on your progress is keeping a diary of your daily actions and noting the results.

Law Number One "As you sow, so shall you reap" is so simple and so true that most of us fail to follow it or realize its power; therefore, take the Golden Square of Paul Omar. Plant it in your mind as a reminder of this law. Let it help to make that peculiar mind of yours act to your advantage.

XIX

THE UNITY OF
SOUL POWER

There is nothing more beneficial than someone's having confidence in you and nothing more wholesome than your having confidence in someone else. Sometimes even pretended confidence works miracles.

Forty years ago in a small town, a street faker was selling a mysterious concoction, to which he gave the high-sounding name of "The Elixir of Life." According to the lecture which preceded the sale, the concoction would cure all the pains and aches to which mankind is heir. To attract a crowd, within the circle of light from the flaring torches on his gaudily painted wagon, he would give a talk on phrenology, illustrating his points with the aid of a human skull and such small-boy subjects as he could induce to assist him.

Arriving at the particular time in his phrenological discussion when he required a human subject to operate upon, he called for volunteers. After a moment's hesitation, a small, unkempt figure mounted the steps that led to the wagon-bed and stopped beside him. With good-natured ridicule, the crowd nudged one another and laughed hilariously. The "subject" who had volunteered was the son of Pete, the village drunkard, probably regarded as the sorriest specimen of the rising generation in the town. "If he's got any bumps on his head," said a voice near me, "the old man put 'em there with a club."

The boy stood blinking in the light of the torches. He was plainly nervous and ill at ease, yet there was a certain touch of courage in his daring this publicity that caught my fancy.

The phrenologist, knowing the psychology of crowds, was quick to take advantage of this opportunity to play upon the humor of his audience. His nimble fingers searched over the boy's head, he turned him this way and that, he tilted his chin, then lowered it, keeping up a running fire of comment and explanation which convulsed the bystanders. . . . "Here is a rare specimen . . . mental, motive type, a student, an executive, a leader . . . benevolent, courageous, industrious, forceful, dominant."

So he rambled on until he saw that the crowd wearied

of the jest; then he abruptly dismissed the boy and turned enthusiastically to the sale of "Elixir of Life." The villagers watched him but I watched the boy, and it seemed to me there was a new look on his face, a new light in his eyes, as though a dormant power within him had been awakened.

He slipped from my sight and the incident was forgotten.

This last summer, I visited the old town again. A street faker held forth in the square. So identical was he with the one of long ago that the incident of the boy came back to me. I turned to the "old inhabitant" who was with me. "By the way," I asked, "whatever became of old Pete's boy?"

He laughed.

"Funny thing, that," he replied. "Ever hear of the Hon. Henry Porter Donnellson who's made such a stir at the Capitol as representative of the State's big business interests? Well, that's him."

What looked like a shabby trick played on old Pete's son was a joke to everyone but the boy. Strange to say, he believed it. Some one had confidence in him, and he was to be a big man as predicted.

My friend, Tim Thrift, who told me this story, added, "Drop a pebble into a placid pool and the ripple of it travels in ever-widening circles to its farthest edge. Drop a thought into a receptive mind and the effect of it for good or ill permeates in ever-increasing measure to its farthest mental horizon."

When Mohammed told Kadijah, his wife, of his vision of heaven and his divine appointment, strange as it may seem, she believed him and was his first convert. Her confidence in Mohammed strengthened his belief and was greatly responsible for the success of the religion he founded.

How true this is and how fortunate, indeed, is the child with parents sensible enough to prophesy a bright future for him or her instead of emphasizing shortcomings. Such parents do not consider the devastating effect of these negative suggestions planted in the alert and fertile mind of the child.

A united soul desire of parent and child for a future success in the life of that child cannot fail to bring such a condition into reality.

The power of suggestion from one mind to another especially when the subject of the suggestion is agreeable and desirable to both, instantly contacts with both souls and a united soul desire is the result.

A prominent Rotarian, now living in Phoenix, Ariz., recently told me the following story about himself:

"One day when I was about sixteen years of age, while I was sitting on a bench watching two teams practice before starting a baseball game, I was talking to a catcher for the St. Louis Browns by the name of Buzz Keck, who had his finger broken and who was spending his time at home in De Soto, Mo., waiting for his finger to heal. He was the idol of all the boys who played ball.

"One of the players on the home team had his finger broken in practice and the captain of the team came over where we were sitting and said to the professional to whom I was talking: 'We sure have some tough luck. The game is ready to start and we have no player to put in the place of our shortstop.'

"The professional said, 'This kid is the best shortstop in the State. Put him in there.'

"Then turning to me, he said, 'Go under the grand stand, put on your suit and show them how to play that position.'

"I went into the game and got along all right until my time came to bat. The professional was sitting beside me and I said to him, 'This is a hard place for me to come up to bat. There are two men on bases and they are going to walk this fellow to get a chance at me and I will come up with the bases full.'

"He said, 'It is the best place in the world for you to come up, as anybody can hit the ball when there is no one on base but it takes a real batter to go up with the bases full and bring them in and you can do it. Remember he has to throw three strikes over the plate and you only have to hit one. No pitcher can throw three over without your hitting one of them. Remember also, that either you are afraid of him or he is afraid of you. *Don't* be in a hurry to get to the plate. Stand outside of the batter's box, spit on your hands, tighten up your belt and laugh at him. Let him know that you are not afraid of him and you'll have the best of it. Let the first ball go by and keep laughing at him. He is not as good as the kids you have been playing with and you are the best batter in the world at your age.'

"I went to bat with the idea that I was the best batter. I hit a two-bagger and scored all three runs. I played against the same pitcher several times afterwards and he often told me he would sooner pitch against anybody else as I was always laughing at him and gave him a great deal of trouble.

"That great lesson of boyhood has been remembered in every walk of my life to this day. It shows what confidence will do and how it is strengthened by the confidence and suggestion of another."

How few realize the great power of suggestion. Take a family of four, living independently of the desires of each other and the result is a disorganized, wrangling, unhappy group, each sincerely believing that one or all of the other three are responsible for the condition. There is little, if any, accomplishment by any one of the four and they would be much better off living separately unless the situation is corrected.

Another family of four living for one another, each knowing and agreeing with the desires of the others, represent a soul strength sixteen times as powerful as the first family mentioned. Each individual is accomplishing progress with the assistance of the other three. The entire family progresses because of soul unity.

When you can get some one "pulling" for you, believing in you, hoping and affirming your success, your chances are twice as good. You secure this, of course, by giving in like kind to others.

The united good-will of its customers is one of the greatest assets of a business because in unity there is always strength.

To obtain genuine benefits it is not sufficient merely to consolidate physical assets. The soul desire of executives, employees, distributors and customers must be focused on a center of common interest. The success or failure of any business depends upon the opinion (soul desire) of all the people it touches.

Both advertising and propaganda are used solely to secure mass approval in affairs of business, cities, states, nations and, in fact, of the whole world.

XX

THE LAW OF MAJORITY

The character of the world is the result of the soul expression of the world and as soul is amenable to mind, naturally, as the world thinketh, so it is. As a nation, state, city or business thinketh, so it is, and thus the Second Law in the Philosophy of Paul Omar reads:

Law Two

"A united soul desire of a majority of the souls affected by the desire becomes a reality."

The desire may not be for the BEST interests of the whole but if the majority of the whole want it and are united in that want, the soul of the whole swayed by the majority brings the desire into reality.

Sometimes the propaganda of a few "pulls the wool" over the eyes of the many. Thus is created a desire for something which benefits only the few who originated the propoganda. People say: a minority rules. Better say: only a minority thinks with reason.

You remember the peroration of Lincoln's Gettysburg Address: "That this nation, under God, shall have a new birth of freedom, and that government of the people, by the people and for the people shall not perish from the earth."

Law Number Two affirms the abiding truth of Lincoln's immortal words: that under God's law, government, in its finality, is and was and always will be of and by and for the people. The question of whether such government is good or bad does not enter into the operation of the law.

Law Number Two deals with unity of souls, two souls or all souls in existence; the soul of a business organization, the soul of a village, city, state or nation.

Many soul desires affect only two persons, or a small group.

Sometimes the desire is the most horrible persecution but the law operates with unfailing accuracy.

The frenzied persecution of witchcraft at Salem is an example.

XXI

SHALL "GOSSIP" HURT OR HELP

Gossip is the most common method of propaganda, creating soul desire of the small group. There is a natural impulse in people to repeat what they hear. Rumors are started and like the pebble thrown into the pond fly to the farthest edge.

Gossip is of two kinds, helpful and hurtful. The first is capable of producing beneficial results, improvement, good will and profit; the second, of inflicting injury, oppression, deterioration and loss.

When James Nason landed in Cedar Falls with his wife and two children, they were met at the depot by Rollins, the chauffeur for Dudly Kahn, president of the plant where Nason was to be head bookkeeper, at the modest salary of eighty-five dollars a month and house furnished.

At the new home, they met their "guardian angel," Mary Gilroy, general help-woman of the exclusive set in Cedar Falls and self-styled "cateress de luxe." "Good-news Mary"—as she was called—knew every one worth while; and, better yet, was loved by all because of her never-failing cheerfulness and an inexhaustible supply of good-news gossip.

In less than a month every one in the village knew that the Nasons were lovely—Mary saw to that. The only apparent flaw lay in the fact that neither Mr. nor Mrs. Nason attended church. The children had entered the Sunday-school and stood well in their classes. The boy soon became librarian of the music and books, and the girl, an active member of the Junior League.

A year later, Mary tipped off the reason why the parents did not go to church: "Mr. Nason is English, you know; he's very proud and he won't go unless he can contribute along with the rest. They're lovely people and so conscientious." The next month, Nason was solicited to take charge of the accounts of the church at a fee, which he promptly refused to do except on one condition: that the fee be returned to the church as his contribution. This, of course, was quite satisfactory.

That was the beginning of Nason's advance. Next, he took charge of the books and records of the Community

Center. This work not only paid his contribution to that activity but gave him a close contact with a majority of the parents and children in the community. He became one of the most popular citizens.

"It would be a wonderful thing for you to have a car"; suggested Mary Gilroy to Mrs. Nason one day. "Why don't you have one?"

"We will some day, perhaps," was the reply, and Mary built her good news on this: "Some day the Nasons will have a car"; and before the summer was over, Charlie Brown, Buick agent, traded in a bargain. Then he went to Nason and the terms were such that Sunday morning saw the Nasons arrive at church in a very attractive coupe. Mary Gilroy was more delighted than the Nasons, if that were possible.

It is now twelve years since Mary Gilroy first started her Good-News Gossip about the Nasons. James Nason has a private office at the plant and underneath his name on the door is "Vice-President and Treasurer." Even the town of Cedar Falls has prospered, due greatly to the Good-News Gossip of Mary Gilroy, the happiest and most successful of its towns-people. The success spoken of is not measured by dollars and cents, but in leadership for good.

About the time the Nasons moved to Cedar Falls, another episode had its beginning in a far eastern city. John Harrison, experimental engineer, had for months worked long hours on a perplexing transmission problem. His theories seemed logical but there was a flaw somewhere.

Jefferson Godfrey, head of the sales department, was a cruel, boisterous, unsympathetic go-getter, hiring and firing those he liked or disliked. He had earned his position by consistent hard work, mingled with a plentiful supply of shrewd politics and crafty tact. His disgust for John Harrison and for his failure to produce the equipment needed was manifest on every occasion. "Listen to me," he would say, "that man Harrison is just a plain nut. He should be put in a cage. He's CRAZY, I tell you!"

This affirmation was made not once but many times. Poor Harrison quite likely wasn't entirely himself; the long hours and worry were telling on him.

One day, when leaving the factory, his mind occupied by other things, he pushed outward on the street door which opened in. The guard at the door saw him and having heard the out-bursts of Godfrey repeated by others, enlarged upon this event. His story of Harrison's strange actions went the rounds. The crew were actually sorry that "John had gone dippy" (that's about the way it was expressed) and in less than a year John was actually in an asylum where he died a few years later.

This is by no means the end of this true story. Five years later, Godfrey, at the height of his success, began to act queerly, was requested to take a leave-of-absence and rest for a year; but his domineering and unreasonable mind would not hear of it. Finally resigned entirely, soon lost his wealth, and he, too, was placed in a private sanitarium, dying a year later.

Common sense tells you not to believe that the cause was unity of thought or soul power. You gladly agree with the Nason story because it turns out beautifully, but the Harrison case is too horrible for you to accept. Warm impulse says "no." Cold reason, however, says "yes."

Nothing on earth could induce you to print in bold letters on the family mirror: "Our baby will die this year." Why not? Because it might HAPPEN, especially if many absorbed the thought printed.

It is an exceedingly poor law which will not work both ways and these true stories illustrate the effect of unity of thought in creating soul desire in small groups. May they also "burn home" the crime of hurtful gossip.

There should be no doubt concerning the truth of the operation of Law Two in your smallest group of associates. Lavator quotes: "A frequent intercourse and intimate connection between two persons make them so alike that not only their dispositions are moulded like each other but their very faces and tones of voice contact a certain analogy," and Shakespeare says: "It is certain that either wise bearing or ignorant carriage is caught as men take disease, one of another. Therefore, let men take heed of their company."

Society is formed by affinities. Judgment is largely formed in conversation with your associates.

The soul desire of your group becomes a reality for the group and you. It is, therefore, prudent to frequent the society of your superiors and make your life wholesomely progressive in the association of great men and good books.

This is, indeed, good counsel to any young reader, as it is self-evident no advancement can be made by association with those who know less than you.

"Things bad begun make strong themselves by ill."

—SHAKESPEARE.

"We shape ourselves, the joy or fear
Of which the coming life is made,
And fill our future's atmosphere
With sunshine or with shade."

—WHITTIER.

XXII

WILL YOU LIMIT GOD'S SUPPLY?

❧

The strength of a group or nation is not measured by number but by unity of purpose (soul desire of the majority). So with the world. Sixty-six nations have ratified the Kellogg-Briand renunciation of War Treaty, hailed as the greatest modern step in outlawry of war. With proper and continued publicity, the majority of souls in these sixty-six nations may firmly unite in the desire for peace. The reality of peace under such a condition is unquestionable and peace would continue until the majority desired otherwise.

The soul, character and life of a nation is the reflection of the thoughts and actions of the majority of the particles of which it is composed. The soul of a nation is affected in the same manner as the soul of an individual. The soul is constantly directing the actions of life, which cannot stand still. There is no stopping place, no top or bottom to the ladder of life.

When a nation or an individual becomes wealthy and powerful, it is in grave danger. Christ said, "Verily, I say unto you, a rich man shall hardly enter into the kingdom of heaven." Surely, the accumulation of any sort of material objects, worthless rocks or valuable ores, diamonds, money, lands, bits of broken glass or bright pebbles could not of itself have any bearing on the subject; but it could and generally does affect with telling results the mind of man or nation. A top may have been reached and there is no top for the soul. Life must be going in some direction and if the mind is satisfied with the heights reached and does not direct the soul in what to do, the life of the nation or individual becomes like a ship without a rudder, ending on the rocks of destruction. Majority rules; therefore, a so-styled self-sufficient man or nation becomes a minority and cannot advance.

What star shines brightest at the top of your "ladder of desire?" When you reach it, what then? You will have to select another, higher up, to strive for or else go down as so many do, carried swiftly along in the current of vanity, self-sufficiency and minority.

The amount placed upon the price mark of success by most of us is ridiculously low, when we stop to think of it: just a little power over a few; just a few more dollars than our neighbors and we reach our heights of success.

Do not pass this statement too quickly, as it is of *vast* importance. There is in the mind of most individuals a hope for success; a hope to reach the top; and how many there are who become self-sufficient, vain and of no value, whatever, to the world, with only a taste of the bounteous supply of success God has prepared for all.

Joe Boescher, eighteen-year-old apprentice, became a junior salesman at twenty-one. His salary increased during this period from $50 to $150 a month. At twenty-two he was made a senior salesman on commission basis. Within a very short time he sold, unassisted and with much credit to himself, the largest single order ever received by his company to that date. The commission amounted to over $2000. Joe reached his top—the height of his desire—as many others have and will.

In spite of good advice from his sales manager and others interested in the success of this bright young man, Joe could not think of any further progress. He had arrived, he was good—he knew it—and needed no advice from any one. He was self-sufficient. He purchased a small car and hired a chauffeur—at least the sales manager said so. Joe called the chauffeur his "junior salesman" but, nevertheless, for several months he lolled in magnificence on the back seat while the chauffeur drove—and sales dropped off.

It was about ten years ago when Joe reached his top, arriving at the bottom two years later. He is now with another firm in a different line at a salary of $125 a month.

Are you sure this could not happen to you? Of course you are; but have a care—it is such an easy matter for most humans to reach the top round of the ladder of desire.

XXIII

THE POWER OF HUMILITY

✤

P aul Omar conquered his material top early in life and was on the down-grade until that eventful Sunday in Seattle when he discovered that the fundamentals of mind and soul, the Law of Karma and the Law of Majority were not all. There was another power greater than these. True it was—the fundamentals had been proved to be correct and the two great laws worked with unerring accuracy. His symbol of the golden square had brought the desired result by keeping his mind in the constant direction of his objective goal. The goal itself seemed helpful to the majority, was desired by the majority and so became a reality.

It was all so simple that he began to doubt it. He doubted the benefit and he doubted himself. He had, in fact, reached the end of his mind, having accomplished everything he had set out to do but it was not sufficient. His soul demanded more. Mind—that function of the human brain guided largely by the senses—could not think more.

Lowell expresses this predicament when he says: "It is only the intellect that can be thoroughly and hideously wicked. It can forget everything in the attainment of its aims. It has only one failing which, to be sure, is a very considerable one,—it has no conscience."

Paul Omar knew that the great power he had discovered and proved was a gift to all men from God but his intellect or mind made him forget this and *he* took the credit. His behavior was as idiotic as simple Joe Boescher's. He even forgot the law of Karma: "take and it will be taken away; give and it will be given back." HE TOOK THE CREDIT OF POWER—and he knew he had lost his power. In his bewilderment and shame, fearing the loss of his intellect or mind, he forgot his self-sufficiency for the moment and called upon his soul for assistance. "God grant me peace" was his prayer.

He was, at the time, in a structure dedicated to God, surrounded by many souls united in devotion to God. There may have been little, if any, unity of mind belief in the song which had preceded his talk; yet there was a unity of mind understanding in the words "Come, Holy Ghost, our souls inspire" and, regardless of the interpretation of what happened to him, his soul received a message which has carried past the threshold of his consciousness, giving him the peace he desired and satisfying the demand of his soul. He had a higher goal to achieve and it was not of this world. The power, greater than all he had discovered was THE SPIRIT OF GOD. When he had acknowledged GOD as the source of power, he received the spirit of God and power because ONE SOUL AND GOD IS A MAJORITY.

It is the privilege of any man to force his soul to act as if there were no God. He can, if he chooses, mentally believe such a situation to be a fact. He can believe that life on this earth is all there is for him and, according to the philosophy of Paul Omar, that becomes a reality for such as so choose. But, believing that the vast majority who have read, thus far, accept the fact that there IS a God who created this world, the stars and the millions of other worlds we mentally know to exist, is it not foolish even to *suggest* that such a God, capable of these wonders, does not control his creations? Is it not also foolish, even to our limited minds, to suggest an absence of purpose in His so creating and controlling?

Every consciously-directed endeavor has an objective or purpose. There is a reason for the action—some result is to be obtained. The law of Karma indicates that God wants man to do only that which is pleasing to man. The law of majority indicates that unity of purpose is another desire of His.

Doing those things which are pleasing to each other creates a love for one another. A unity of the majority in so doing binds a people together in love, with each man interested in the welfare of his brother, and establishes the operation of the spirit of God—a power for good greater than all others.

The history of man as told in the Bible, or any accurate history of man or nation, indicates clearly that when the majority are not functioning according to the purpose of God, something happens. The spirit of God takes a hand in the procedure and corrects the situation.

Let no one—man or nation—boast that he stand, lest he fall. Success, wealth, power, and man taking the credit for it, brought on a pride and vanity which caused our world war—the result of which is an example of divine interference in the affairs of men which should not soon be forgotten; but, unfortunately, the mind of man forgets quickly.

When the spirit of God in man becomes manifest on this earth, by a majority, the Kingdom of God on earth which Christ prophesied will become a reality.

Paul Omar assumes "soul" to be the God-given man-power—the power which changed water into wine and raised the dead; while "spirit" in man is the purpose of God released in him, making truth and love in his life, and making you what in your unselfish moments you long to be—perfect in the Spirit of a God your soul knows to exist.

Spirit is that something you long for and cannot define and which, if once secured, completely satisfies you. Spirit is eternal, soul being an intermediate between the material and the spiritual. You may by soul power gain the spirit of God, or accept falseness and death.

"For as in Adam all die" (I Cor. 15:22) meant to Omar that man by sins, such as Adam committed, lost his Spirit. "Even so in Christ shall all be made alive" meant that Christ—God in man's form—showed by human example the way to regain the Spirit and also sent the Holy Ghost as a comforter and guide to truth. The good and true in you is Spirit—and the good and true of the universe is the Spirit of God.

Just what God's ultimate objective is for man may not be made known to us,—but we do know, intuitively, by messages from the soul—

"that there is a life beyond the death of the body and that our spirit goes on to take its place in another world and

that the kind of life lived on this earth will make a difference in the possible opportunities in the life beyond!

"There will be a continuation of personal identity. The limitations of human life will be removed and an infinitely closer knowledge of God will be possible. There will be progress and development and there will be active service of a broader sphere.

"For such an immortality there is a universal seeking implanted in the heart of humanity in all ages. The idea was in the process of development during the Old Testament times; it was completed in the Christian gospel and it was established by the fact of the resurrection of our Lord, Jesus Christ.

"As to the 'how' of it, as the 'where' or whether there will be any 'where' about it, as to what people will look like, how they will talk, what they will do—Christianity professes a reverent ignorance." (Quoted from "Common Sense Religion.")

XXIV

GIVE THE GLORY TO GOD

God has given you a soul capable of any accomplishment—and a mind to direct that soul. You can have what you want: health, power, wealth and eternal life, but the human mind is so fickle and wicked that such gifts have proved disastrous to many.

> *"If drunk with sight of power we loose*
> *Wild tongues that have not Thee in awe;*
> *Such boastings as the Gentiles use*
> *Or lesser breeds without the law—*
> *Lord God of Hosts, be with us yet*
> *Lest we forget—lest we forget."*

So cautions Kipling in his famous "Recessional" and so the Third Law of this Philosophy reads:

LAW THREE
"The glorification of God is necessary to continued or eternal advancement."

This means, in simple words, to give God the credit, the glory and the thanks for your successful accomplishments and, further, to blame your method of thinking for life's misfortunes.

God is Love and the power of love is the power of God. If you could understand this fully you would understand life eternal but the power of God (love) is beyond human understanding. The best we can do, with our human minds, is to use the great powers God has given us in expressing His purpose as we see it and glorify Him in thought, word and deed.

You, individually, can possess the Spirit of God by continually giving out of the never-ending supply of love God gives to you. This, however, is not enough—you must also unite with others and increase by unity the Spirit and purpose of God on earth.

Unity is the elemental virtue and foundation of religious life and, therefore, the church of God is a necessity to advancement.

"Glory to God in the Highest—and on earth Peace, Good Will toward men." THAT is the MEANING OF THE MARK of Paul Omar—the Cross of Jesus Christ, an ever-present reminder that the glory belongs to God; and the square of humanity below it to remind us of that love we must necessarily give our fellow man in order to live in the fullness of God's love.

If you can interpret the meaning of this mark—and live it as does Paul Omar—you will be filled with abundance of health, wealth and happiness and, above all, a positive intelligence that you are training your spirit for an active and purposeful life to come which will be eternal according to God's plan.

So endeth the second version of the MEANING OF THE MARK; but there may be some among you unable to put into practise the wonderful truths set forth in the story and explanations. For such, a third version, based somewhat upon the application of the "Mark of Success" and the philosophy it suggests, follows.

VERSION
III

XXV

THREE MEN——THREE AGES——ONE THOUGHT

In the study of scientific salesmanship, you will find this important rule: In order to have the prospect fully understand the value of the goods or service you have for sale, three steps are necessary: first, tell him what you intend to tell him; second, tell him; third, tell what you have told him.

In this third interpretation of the Meaning of the Mark of success, you will be told in a different way what you have already been told in the first and second versions. This is for the benefit of the thousands whose minds react through an appeal to the emotions with such intensity that soul-accomplishment occurs without apparent reason or cause.

There is, however, A REASON AND A CAUSE WHICH

MUST BE KNOWN IN ORDER TO FORM A PERMANENT SYSTEM OF ADVANCEMENT.

Several months ago I read a little circular, printed on blue paper, and signed by a man of whom I had never heard. The closing paragraph indicated that his business had to do with getting orders and the only apparent intent of this piece of printed matter was to encourage many struggling individuals in his line of endeavor.

The substance of the contents of this circular follows:

"For as he thinketh in his heart so is he." —SOLOMON.

"There is nothing either good or bad but thinking makes it so." —SHAKESPEARE.

"No man sinks in the waters of fate except one cramped with fear. Kick and you will float." —W. C. DUNLAP.

Here, my friends, we find three men saying the same thing.

King Solomon lived thirty-five hundred years ago. He was the RICHEST, the most PROSPEROUS and the WISEST man of his time.

The second statement, by Shakespeare, was made

about three hundred and fifty years ago. In his plays and poems he left for all generations a legacy of keen penetration and shrewd revelation of human nature that has never been surpassed.

Mr. W. C. Dunlap is an outstanding example of the modern big man, with a big job in a big corporation.

Three men, representing three ages, all saying the same thing in different words. Aren't their utterances deserving of attention and thought?

Physically, these three men resemble you and me—two legs, two arms, a body, ears to hear with, eyes to see with, a mouth to talk with and a *brain to think with*. That is the point—A BRAIN TO THINK WITH.

Our good friends, the M.D.'s, tell us that the average human male brain weighs fifty ounces. There is little variation. The difference in weight between the brain of the down-and-out bum and that of the scientist or business leader is only a few ounces. Sounds mysterious, doesn't it? Not at all. The only difference between that down-and-out bum and that scientist or business leader is a *difference in the way they use their brain*.

What are YOU going to use YOUR brains for? What am I going to use MY brains for? You can't decide that for me. Neither can I decide it for you. But you *must* agree that no amount of argument or speculation can alter the fact that "As he thinketh in his heart so is he."

Are you going to think: "It can't be done"; "I can't do it"; "I am afraid of this"; "I am afraid of that"? Shucks and rubbish! my friend. They sell ash cans to put that stuff in.

I don't know what You are going to think but I know what I am going to keep on thinking.

I am going to keep on thinking up new, simpler and better ways whereby "it CAN be done"; newer, simpler and better ways of approaching people and influencing them toward right thinking, which produces prosperity and happiness.

Folks *like* to have you approach them with this attitude. They will *thank* you for it. Yes, they will thank you both in words and WITH ORDERS. Fear? It isn't there, it doesn't exist.

—C. F. Wyant,
Minneapolis, Minn.

Will you do as Mr. Wyant suggests and, by using your mind correctly, eliminate this self-created fear?

Mr. Dunlap's editorials concerning business-building methods are published on a national scale. He directs a large sales force, is actively engaged in many local and national civic organizations, but with all this is not too busy to write one or more mind-building editorials each week. This is his contribution to humanity. An editorial appears later in this volume.

XXVI

LIMITLESS SUPPLY

Why not expose yourself to success? Train your mind not to believe all your senses tell you. Imagine *perfect* conditions. Affirm what you wish to exist. Tell yourself that the things you want *already* exist for you in limitless supply. This may seem foolish to the reasoning mind but you will find it works in the same mysterious way as do all the wonders of God.

Quit brooding and worrying about things you fear may happen. Train your mind to think correctly of Good and wonders will constantly unfold to your reason. You cannot be successful or happy when in misery which, together with every undesirable condition in life, is caused by lack of harmony with good; in other words,—caused by being out of tune with God and your fellow man.

The mysterious Mark of Success is the tuning key, but before receiving instructions in its use you must know about the cause and effect of correct thinking. Correct thinking causes correct action which brings about a body-and-soul harmony with good, thus forming the foundation for success and happiness.

Your mind, which does the thinking, is controlled greatly by the five senses. What you see, hear, feel, taste and smell is instantly made known to you through the mind. The thoughts of your mind are in constant contact with your soul, the power which governs every action of your life. The soul puts into existence or action what the mind suggests. For this reason, a man's environment and associates have greatly to do with the kind of life he lives, his success and his happiness.

The mind of man is by no means entirely controlled by the five human senses. The soul of man also suggests intuitively to the mind and an unspoken word or phrase becomes a thought unrelated to the senses. Therefore, correct thinking, causing correct actions, bringing to you success and happiness, may be achieved only by correct environment of the five senses, the correct interpretation of the intuitive suggestions of the soul and the correct unspoken word or phrase.

The definition of correct thinking for our purpose is:

"thoughts which are harmoniously agreeable to God and man as a whole."

Thoughts agreeable to God come to you through the intuitive messages from your soul, often intensified by the senses. Thoughts agreeable to man come to you more frequently through the senses and are often intensified by intuition. Words and phrases spoken and unspoken are the beginning of action, life and realities.

XXVII

A RITUAL OF ATTAINMENT

How can you get that habit-contaminated mind of yours working in harmony with good and success and happiness?

Bill Jones, quick on the trigger, ready for an argument or a fight at all times, placed in his office that beautiful, peaceful, blue picture, entitled "Daybreak" by Parrish, in a position where he was forced to look at it when using the telephone. The picture, working through the sense of sight, suggested beauty, peace and harmony. The telephone conversations improved by harmonizing with the picture and Bill's friends and business increased.

His desk, as well as that of his secretary, was always untidy; so he arranged for a small vase of fresh flowers to be placed on each desk daily. Beautiful flowers do not harmonize with disordered papers, hence the result was—two tidy, well-arranged desks.

A bright and cheerful phonograph record, played while he ate breakfast, started him off for work whistling this tune and seeing a blue sky on a rainy day.

In this same manner your five human senses create thousands of thoughts daily which are relayed to your soul and, if unrestrained, make your life subject entirely to what you see, hear, feel, taste or smell.

You positively know that such a life could not be productive of success or happiness. The intuitive messages from your soul tell you there is something of greater worth; otherwise life could not be worth the living. Let us tune in with "that something" we know to exist.

Do this: Take your pencil and make the sign of the Cross of Christ Jesus. Have you done that? Look at this symbol steadfastly and say, "Thanks be unto God for His unspeakable gift (II Cor. 9:15). Glory to God in the highest." . . . Did you say that, and did you mean it? Repeat it for good measure. Burn this thought into your mind until it dominates the thoughts created by the senses, thus forming a contact with your soul which is the power God gave you. Now say, "I give Almighty God, my Father, all the credit and all the glory for this power He has given me as revealed in Christ." Say it again. Try to *mean* it, When You Really Mean It, You Will Feel the Power of God In You.

Now make the sign of the square. Look at it steadfastly for at least a minute. Make this silent vow: "By this symbol I will ever remember to do unto my fellow man as I would he should do unto me."

When you have allowed this vow to sink deep into your inner consciousness, say: "My God, my Father, I love you and I know you love me because it is your will that I be perfect in every way. Only by not believing this am I denied its fulfillment. Lord I believe. Help Thou my unbelief."

Do this at every opportune time, in silence and alone except for the presence of God, until you can feel His presence. Some day you will see His presence in every flower, star, cloud and every object of vision; in every sound, touch, smell and taste. You will become conscious of His nearness and oneness to you.

If perchance, about this time in your reading, you should hear that vagabond mind of yours say "Old stuff! I've heard all this before"—do not be discouraged. Don't give up. Go back and read it all over again because you are being told of a method by which you can gain the Whole World, and by egotistically taking the credit, may lose a million years of soul progress. Do not let your sense-controlled mind rob you of the great divine gift of soul guidance.

Keep the cross of Christ and the square of humanity ever before you as you go on.

"Glory and credit to God in the highest and on earth peace, good will toward man." As the Great Teacher said, "Render unto Caesar the things that are Caesar's and to God the things that are God's."

With glory to God and good will toward man, you eliminate fear and can, without worldly-wisdom contradiction say: "The power of God within me is possible of every accomplishment."

A boy going to school is in need of a reference book in order to progress with his studies. His father is the source of supply in purchasing the book. The boy knows his father is interested in his progress at school, so he comes to his father and says that he needs the book. He tells where it can be obtained, the reason for the need of it and how much it will cost. He does not beg for it or demand it. He simply states his requirements and the father, understanding them, arranges for the boy to secure the book.

In the same manner are you to go to your Heavenly Father and state the facts concerning YOUR requirements.

Your mind needs considerable assistance, so get out your pencil again and a sheet of paper. At the top make the sign of the cross and square. The reason is obvious by now. Next, write down your first and most important desire; the reason for it is important; why you desire it and where it can be obtained. Seek the opinion of your soul as to the value of this possession and do not demand it. When you have completed a thorough survey of the desire, finish by writing, "Thy will, O God, not mine, be done. Direct me and I will follow."

The result will be as God wills, and you are in no danger as you have placed the matter in His hands. If you are sincere and will follow the suggestion of your soul, the desire will become a reality and at the very time expected; or else you will have good reason for not wanting it.

That there be no misconstruction of what has just been said, let it be stated that apparently God does not interfere with the soul desires of individuals except by request. It is being demonstrated constantly that humans are desiring and securing by soul power conditions contrary to God's plan for them. For this reason is suggested the symbol of the mark of Paul Omar as a guide to correct thinking, correct desires and God-pleasing accomplishments.

> *"One thing I know, that whereas I was blind, now I see"* (John 9:25), *replied he, that was blind, to the questions of the Pharisees. It is sincerely believed that before this volume is finished, you will say likewise.*

XXVIII

TO OBTAIN WEALTH

Your mind does not necessarily have to believe at the start of your experiment but you cannot become wealthy when constantly talking, thinking and acting poverty. You cannot accumulate wealth by association with those who are poor and always expect to be. Therefore, change your environment, your thoughts, actions and talk. In this way you unconsciously secure the assistance of the five senses in forming a dominant wealth-thought. Prepare for wealth. See it already yours in limitless supply. Spend some money. Get out of the pinching-the-penny habit.

Several years ago a salesman explained to me that he would have to quit his job. Sales were dropping off; he owed the company for advanced commissions; the grocer's bill was unpaid and the rent was two months past due. I explained to him that there was plenty of money in his town, only he was on the wrong side of it—recommending that he use his persuasive salesmanship on the boss for one hundred dollars additional advance and to spend the money as instructed.

It is surprising what a modish dress his wife secured for fifteen dollars and what a chic hat for five dollars. A new suit, hat, shoes and tie were his purchases and that evening, with thirty-five dollars in real money, this couple "stepped out" just as though it was the customary thing for them. They had a real dinner at one of the best eating houses. He bought two good cigars and tipped the waiter one dollar. They then went to a show and when it was over were about to take a taxi home when a gentleman said to the salesman: "Good evening, Mr. Jones. Would you mind letting me have this taxi? My wife is not feeling so well."

"Sure thing," said Jones.

"And by the way," said the man, "see me at the office tomorrow. The deal you suggested is about ripe."

Jones and wife walked home "on air"—a new man and woman. They really felt and acted as if business was good. The commission on the deal, closed before noon the next day, was over four hundred dollars and Jones snapped out of his slump by investing one hundred dollars in Prosper-ity Actions. He has never slumped since and is at present a large stockholder and acting head of a milling company in the suburbs of Cincinnati.

You can readily understand that Jones could have spent this one hundred dollars and remained in the slump; but, on the other hand, it would have been almost impossible for him to secure the assistance of his senses in attaining a prosperity attitude without funds.

If you really want prosperity, Act It—Live It—Think It—and It Is Yours. There is an unlimited supply to draw from. Get out the pencil, put down the amount you want and work out an honorable plan intuitively agreeable to your soul for securing it. Follow the plan and the amount is yours—at the time you planned for it. Simple enough, isn't it?

Play fair with yourself, with God and your fellow man. Try it.

XXIX

TO OBTAIN HEALTH

Are you ill? Are you *sure* of it? God never intended you to be so but if you know you are then something should be done about it.

The following news item taken from one of the big Dailies is interesting and is food for thought:

"This is a snake story to keep one up nights—and sober. It was brought into New York today by Allan A. Lonnberg, vice-president of the Grace Line.

"The Grace liner 'Santa Rita,' on which Lonnberg was a passenger from Valparaiso, Chile, put in on July 7th at the port of Guayaquil, Ecuador. Mr. Lonnberg went ashore.

"Shortly before midnight he heard a tremendous clamor in the town. Police were called out, the militia thronged down the narrow streets, fire engines clanged over the cobbles.

"Mr. Lonnberg followed the procession to the edge of town, where the jungle begins and where is located the Civil hospital.

"A ten-foot boa constrictor had glided out of the undergrowth and made its entrance into the hospital through a window. Gliding down corridor after corridor, it finally got into the cripples' ward. Night lights were burning. Some one screamed.

"Then, all at once, panic reigned and shrieks of fright and hysteria rent the air. The snake had attacked a male nurse. The cripples, many of them bedfast for months, leaped from their beds and fled on newly vitalized limbs to the windows.

"One man who had been paralyzed for more than two years jumped six feet, from his bed to a window, and another eight feet to the hospital's patio.

"Doctors, examining him later, believed him cured. His had been a hysterical paralysis.

"The police and militia killed the snake."

In the year of 1904 there lived in Indianapolis, across the street from me, a crippled man of some sixty years of age. He was an early riser and between 6:30 and 7:00 o'clock each morning would, with the assistance of a crutch under the right arm and a cane in the left hand, manage to navigate to the corner, some two-hundred feet away, making the laborious round trip in just about thirty minutes.

I always inquired concerning his health when we met and he invariably replied that he hoped to hold out for the month.

About twelve o'clock one night the whole neighborhood was awakened. The old fellow's house was a mass of flames and we were sure he had perished. Rushing up to the thorough-fare corner to watch for coming fire engines, I came upon the old man, clad only in his night shirt, surrounded by a dozen or so of the neighbors. He was dancing and actually showing how he could kick. "Let 'er burn," was one of his remarks, "I'm cured!"

He had been aroused by the heat, saw the room full of flames, jumped through a window and ran to the corner, sans crutch, sans cane, sans slippers. Bare-footed he had made it in a few jumps. I saw him many times afterwards, walking as well as any man of his age; but he would never discuss the miracle which had happened to him.

The following editorial by W. C. Dunlap, page 55 in his book, "Cheerful Common Sense," is stimulating indeed:

MIND-HEALING

"Dr. Charles Gilbert Davis, a Chicago surgeon, has written a book entitled, 'The Philosophy of Life.' The gist of the book is the influence of thought upon the body, the power of thought to prevent and to cure diseased conditions.

"The thought is not new.

"But the particular value of this book is that this idea is handled by a skilled physician.

"The reasonable man doubts the direct connection between what takes place in thought and what takes place in the body. 'Thought,' says Dr. Davis, 'can produce hunger or destroy appetite; it can cause a chill or a fever; it can make the body perspire; it can dry up the the saliva; it can make the teeth chatter and the eyes swim with tears; it can bring sleep or insomnia; it can slow down the heart till death ensues.'

"From this he continues: 'I believe that it is only necessary to enter upon a course of training and in a brief space of time the results will be seen in improved health.'

"'No living human being need be a chronic invalid repining at fate.'

"'Every hopeful idea created in the mind stimulates the heart, improves digestion and promotes normal action of every gland.'"

"Well, what is your trouble, if any? Surely, no snake or fire is recommended; but healthful thoughts, healthful actions and healthful environment will, by the grace of God in His glorious gift in you, do the healing."

If you are surrounded by sympathetic friends or relatives, you have a double duty to perform. You must convince them as well as yourself that you are daily improving.

Denying the existence of your real or imaginary trouble will only make matters worse. The senses will contradict the statement and your friends, if not openly, will silently do likewise.

Make a MIND PICTURE of yourself wholly perfect, as God wills you to be and say: "This is the way I was intended to be; the way God wants me to be." By doing this you will reflect such a picture on your soul, the correcting process will start and you will see yourself day by day, becoming nearer and nearer the perfect picture until you are entirely whole. Idleness does not harmonize with health; action does.

Get your pencil busy writing plans for work, play and romance when you have become perfect again. Include others in these plans, when possible, because if you can get one or more friends actually to believe in the picture of your perfect health and to be interested in the accomplishment of your future plans, the recovery will be as many times more rapid as the square of the number believing with you.

Jesus Christ said, "Whatsoever ye ask the Father in my name, He will give it you." Put the picture of your perfect self in God's sight, ask in Christ's name and you will be made whole. This statement bears the testimony of millions who have proved it.

Can humanity—when filled with the glory of God and love for all mankind—be anything but perfect in mind, body, soul, spirit and estate? It can not; consequently use the sign of the Cross and square as a symbol to assist your mind in so picturing yourself.

God wills that You be perfect. Your help is necessary to make this a reality.

XXX

TO OBTAIN HAPPINESS

God Is Good and Good Is Happiness

Happiness, like every gift of God, can be avoided only by contrary thinking.

In the room next to my study, a young girl is singing:

"I'm in love with you, Honey;
Say you love me too, Honey.
No one else will do, Honey,
Seems funny, but it's true.
Loved you from the start, Honey;
Bless your little heart, Honey,
Every day would be so sunny, Honey,
With you."

A humanity filled with the Glory of God and love for all mankind can be nothing short of perfect. Such a love fills this little girl at this very moment. God is a part of her happiness. She is thinking love and all is well.

When you can see good in all things you can not fail to be happy; and good means God.

If you have the "croaking" or gloom-spreading habit, you are certainly not in harmony with God. Change your contrary thinking. You're all right and the world's all right. There's a sky of blue above. Sing, dance, fish, hunt, play golf, read, go to the theatre, concert and go to church. Do what your soul tells you a happy man or woman should. Glorify God in your happiness. Love mankind in your joy.

> "Those who joy would win, must share it.
> Happiness was born a twin." —BYRON.

Share it and live it. Think happiness, feel happiness, see happiness, hear happiness, taste happiness and smell happiness in every act of your life. Happiness is so easily secured that it is not even necessary to write down the plan for obtaining it, as has been recommended with other desires.

Be your natural self, good, as God intended you to be and happiness is yours. God's supply of happiness is *overflowing* in you. Take it in the fullness of the Giver and share this abundant blessing with every living thing. HAPPINESS IS YOURS BY DIVINE RIGHT.

XXXI

TO OVERCOME SORROW

From what has been said about happiness, it would seem there should be no sorrow in the world but there can be no denying the fact that sorrow is at times very real. A young wife is taken away from a loving husband and three small children; a boy just finishing college, the pride of his parents and the life of a community, is thrown from a horse to rise no more; a young husband is drowned on his honeymoon.

Sorrow is real to those who loved and are left behind. With perfect health, sufficient wealth, living in a world of happiness, sorrow suddenly knocks at your door. The senses and understanding are of no help to you in such a time.

Real sorrow must be overcome through the unspoken word and the soul's intuitive yet positive answer. In this manner you get a glimpse of a Love beyond understanding.

Christ's sorrow was real but He overcame it.

Wisdom, satisfaction and peace cannot be had except through silent contact with a real personal God. Go alone into a quiet place and there in the silence ask for guidance and wisdom. Do this regularly and at certain periods each day—early morning preferably.

You may need objective assistance. If so, look at the cross of Christ. Silently pray, and eventually your human understanding will make way for the soul's message which will come to you from your Heavenly Father clearly, distinctly and with positive meaning. Fear and doubt will be erased forever and you will, like Paul Omar, go out into God's sunshine with a perfect peace of soul which can not be explained.

To avoid sorrow, to eliminate fear and to live a life of overflowing gladness, you must experience this inner communion with your Creator; seek wisdom, satisfaction and peace in silent communion with your soul.

"Seek and ye shall find." Yea, verily. You will be surprised how quickly you will find. It may be in less than a week of silent prayer, daily, at the same time, that you will feel the strength, power and sureness of divine guidance. Then, surely, before you at all times will be the Meaning of the Mark: Glory to God; good will to man.

XXXII

ALPHA OR OMEGA—— WHICH?

Call what you have read "philosophy," if you like. Call it "religion," if you wish. Call it anything you want. The fact remains that you, yourself, are a power for good or evil. Naturally you desire good but at the same time you are surrounded by evil thoughts, fears and doubts—your own, and those of others.

The Bible is given to us as a guide, the life of Christ as an example; yet thousands upon thousands do not understand the Bible and know not how Christ lived. Ministers, priests, laymen and writers tell such conflicting stories regarding Truth that many of us are lost in the wilderness of ideas. We want something which can be proved and God has given us the proof.

You can prove God's gift of achievement by creating a dominant mind-thought which contacts with your soul and becomes a reality.

Your life is made happy or miserable, healthful or sick, rich or poor, by the way you think. You can be bad or good and have ever with you the faculty of knowing one from the other.

Following what you have read in this volume, forcing your mind to act as you wish it to, writing your desires, reading them, enlarging on the plan of possession, affirming it has come to pass before the worldly mind believes it, going into silence for soul assistance will and does bring into actual reality, the dominant desire. *This you can prove.*

Giving and receiving in the same measure can be proved in less than a minute, although sometimes a greedy, cheating, rotten character seems to progress in power for years before the bill of compensation is presented for payment. It comes, sooner or later, and nothing is more sure than the proof of this law.

Unity with others creates power for good or bad. This we see daily. Egotism, self-importance and self-sufficiency prevent unity of purpose, resulting in loss of power. This has been proved times innumerable, from the fall of man to this day, individually and collectively.

Giving the credit and the glory to God prevents egotism and pride. Thus also, by giving, *we receive*.

The poor old mind is so busy with the multitude of thoughts beating through our senses and souls, together with the activity of millions of other senses and souls, that it seems almost impossible to control it or become centered. ("Centered" means having a home port—a permanent starting and stopping place; a headquarters where you can be found and find yourself; a place of refuge from the flights of imagination, business struggles, doubts and fears.)

Ivan Levine, an uneducated boy, through a peculiar, mysterious thought-wave, connected with an idea which could be proved, was proved and improved by wealth, sorrow, dissatisfaction, and finally, wisdom, satisfaction and peace—centered around a symbol which as Paul Omar, he called the "Price Mark of Success."

Behind this centering symbol, necessary to control his unruly mind, shines the true and glorious center of his life: God, the Father and Creator, to whom all glory must be given; together with man made in His likeness and by grace impelled to unite in love, one for another, thus harmonizing with the plan of eternal advancement.

If you are so disposed, you may at this moment take your pencil and reprice your personal value by making the code symbol of Paul Omar and then, assisted by the sense of vision, feel its true meaning to be a beginning of a new life full of *Wisdom, Satisfaction, Happiness and Peace.*

This may be the end.

It can be the beginning.

The choice is yours.

ABOUT THE AUTHOR

Roy Herbert Jarrett (1874–1937) was a Chicago sales executive and advertising man. After many years of studying metaphysical success methods, Jarrett produced the landmark pamphlet *It Works* in 1926. It has sold more than 1.5 million copies. In 1931, Jarrett followed up his mind-power classic with his second and final book, *The Meaning of the Mark*, which served as the "inner key" to his earlier volume. Long unavailable, *The Meaning of the Mark* is restored to print in this rediscovery volume.

If you enjoyed this book, visit

www.tarcherbooks.com

and sign up for Tarcher's e-newsletter to receive
special offers, giveaway promotions, and
information on hot upcoming releases.

TARCHER
PENGUIN

Great Lives Begin with Great Ideas

Connect with the Tarcher Community

• • •

Stay in touch with favorite authors!
Enter weekly contests!
Read exclusive excerpts!
Voice your opinions!

Follow us

 Tarcher Books

 @TarcherBooks

If you would like to place a bulk order
of this book, call 1-800-847-5515.

Printed in the United States
by Baker & Taylor Publisher Services